I0143088

Ferocious Flirting: Making Marriage Wonderful

Matthew O. Smith

Copyright © 2008 by Matthew O. Smith

Published by The Cleverly Group
Layton, Utah
http://press.cleverly.com

All rights reserved. No part of this publication may be reproduced, stored in a retrieval system, or transmitted, in any form or by any means, electronic, mechanical, photo-copying, recording or otherwise without the prior permission of the author.

ISBN: 978-0-9661731-9-2

Subjects:

- Christian Life—General
- Christian Life & Practice
- Communication in Marriage
- Family & Relationships—General
- Family/Marriage
- General
- Interpersonal Communication
- Interpersonal Relations
- Love
- Love & Romance
- Marriage
- Married People
- Religion
- Self-Help

Dedicated to Janet, my sweetheart.

Thank you to all my readers and especially for your kind and insightful feedback. Special thanks to Michael A. Cleverly whose knowledge, experience and willingness made this book a reality, to Val Chadwick Bagley for providing illustrations to accompany each chapter, and to Rachael Hodson for designing the cover on short notice.

Preface

When my wife and I were married, the man who performed the ceremony gave us this new commandment, "Thou shalt ferociously flirt with thy wife all the days of thy life." As time passed and our family grew, the charge to flirt with my wife was forgotten. Life and marriage became routine. We were caught in the daily drudge.

Then I read an article on the importance of smiling. With work, kids, chores and everything else that demands time and attention, we had forgotten to even flirt enough to smile. Remembering the advice we had received to "ferociously flirt," I set about to flirt more with my sweetheart. Not being a naturally gregarious guy, I studied on ways to flirt with my wife. As I did so, our relationship naturally became stronger and funner.

That was almost 10 years ago. As I worked to understand relationships and how to improve my marriage, I realized that there are lots of people, men and women, seeking to improve their own marriages, trying to find the flame that was just smouldering. The thought occurred to me: Why not share what I have learned and has worked so well in my own marriage?

To this end I created a website, ferociousflirting.com and called it "Romatic Tips for Married Couples." The website now contains over 250 articles dedicated to improving the relationship between a husband and wife. The articles are all family-friendly and each one shares some tip, date idea, or thought on keeping the fire alive.

This book is a collection of many of those first 250 articles from ferociousflirting.com. The website continues to grow with more fun, romantic and informative articles. After reading this book, be sure to check the website for even more ideas and enjoy ferociously flirting with your sweetie.

— Matthew Smith
West Bountiful, Utah
February 14, 2008

i

Table of Contents

Continue Courting

Romantic Bible Verses

Gifts and Surprises

Date Ideas

Valentines

Christmas and Other Holidays

Family

Appendix

Continue Courting

Take Time to Smile

Often, with the demands of work, I come home less than cheerful. With the stress of chores, kids, school, soccer, piano, etc. etc. etc., my wife is also feeling run down by evening. With all the demands on our time and with so many things that need our attention, the nightly greeting between sweethearts can lack warmth. Think about it: You two have spent most of the day apart. With sleep, work, school, sports, and all the other things that happen in a standard day, its very easy to let the whole day pass without a single warm smile or flirtatious touch.

Make the time that you and your sweetie meet after being apart all day a time to smile. First, perpare yourself. If it has been a stressful day, use the last few minutes before you see your sweetie, to start thinking happy thoughts. Maybe remember a happy time you spent with your sweetie.

Now, meeting your sweetheart. Let the first thing your sweetheart sees is a big, happy smile. If it has been a while since you smiled, your sweetie might wonder what you are up to. This is ok, just smile wider and maybe even chuckle. Then say something silly like "I was just thinking of how wonderful it is to be married to the most gorgeous babe on the planet" or "I was just thinking of how jealous all the other girls are that I allowed you to catch me" or some other outragous flirt you can come up with.

Ten seconds spent smiling and flirting can make the whole evening less stressful and more enjoyable for the whole family.

"Look Into My Eyes"

Hold both of her hands and look into your sweetie's eyes. Hold your gaze until your sweetheart starts to wonder what you are up to. At that moment, smile and mouth the words "I love you." Finish it off with a great big bear hug.

Make a Note of It

Throughout the year that special someone in your life will make comments like "oh, I've always wanted one of those," "I just know we could never get that" or "maybe someday...". You get the idea. This is known as hint dropping. When a hint it dropped, make a note of it.

First, get yourself a notepad, or just a page in or day planner or some spot in your PDA. Call it your "hint list." Next, whenever a hint is dropped, log it in the hint list. Then, next time you feel like doing something special, take one of the things off the hint list and make it happen. The fact that you paid attention enough to note the hint and remembered the hint sometime afterward will make you spouse feel even more loved.

Physical Evidence

"Talk is cheap" or so it has been said. In the area of romance, talk may be cheap, but it is also necessary. We all need to hear that we are loved and appreciated. And a sincere expression of gratitude is never wrong. However, hearing is just one of the senses. If you can involve the other senses in the expressions of love and gratitude it will be that much more effective and memorable.

Leave a short note of love and gratitude to be found at a later time, preferably when you are not around. Write the note on something other than just white paper. If possible, include some small treat. This small act will involve four of the five senses: the writing and the paper for the eyes, the feel of the paper and the act of unfolding the note for the sense of touch, the treat for both the taste and smell. When several of the senses are included, the message seems more "real." That is, it seems more sincere and it is therefore more enjoyable and memorable.

You've Got Romance

Send your sweetie a romantic email. Several web sites on the internet allow you to send greetings cards via email. Don't wait for a special occasion, send one just because you are thinking of your sweetheart.

Hug

Touch is an important part of a marriage relationship. Some people suggest that we need eight or more hugs a day for proper sense of self and well-being.

An added benefit is that by giving a hug, you are receiving the same benefit as the recipient. How many hugs have you given your sweetie in the past week? Try to work up to eight in one day and see if it doesn't make you both feel better.

Holding Hands Improved

What is nicer than holding hands? You can do it almost anywhere, almost anytime, while doing most any activity. You can hold hands while walking, waiting, watching, and any time you want to let your sweetie know you are there. If you haven't held hands for a while, try it.

However, even the simple act of holding hands can be improved upon. Next time you are holding hands with your spouse, give three small squeezes. When they look at you, do it again, but this time say "I" with the first squeeze, "love" with the second, and "you" with the third. Now you have a way to tell your sweetheart that you love them whenever you want, even when you doing so outloud would not be appropriate. A private, secret message you can send whenever you want to or your sweetie needs it.

Make 'em Laugh

Do you remember the movie "Singing in the Rain?" The "Make 'em Laugh" scene is one of the most memorable scenes of the whole movie. One of the reasons that it holds up so well is that in today's world of movie-magic and computer effects, is that that scene of dancing and slap-stick is still a joy to watch. I just laugh and say, "How did he do that?" Maybe I should have included "Singing in the Rain" in the romantic movies article (see page 74), but I digress...

Tonight, have a good laugh with your sweetie. While jokes[1] are good for a laugh, a personal anecdote can be even funnier. Better yet is recalling an experience that you and your sweetheart shared. During our honeymoon we were eating at a restaurant and I had spilled ice on the table. The the waitress then looked at me and exclaimed "Slob!" Then she came back with the food and said "Keep it on your plate or in your mouth!" That one still makes us both bust-up laughing whenever we think about it.

---

[1] http://m0smith.freeshell.org/blog-humor

How About a Foot Rub

Most everyone loves to have their feet rubbed. We stand on our feet, walk on them, jump on them and otherwise abuse our feet all day long. It is no surprise that a little pampering of your sweetheart's feet will go a long way toward making your sweetie feel pampered all over. Rubbing them with a nice peppermint lotion just before bed seems to work well. As a matter of fact, there's a method to the whole foot rub. There are those who claim that like acupuncture, reflexology contributes to the health of the whole body. In reflexology, each area of the foot is mapped to some other area of the body. For example if you have a head cold, then rubbing the "sinus" section of the foot, the pads of the toes, is supposed to help. Does it really work? Try it and find out. The worst that could happen is your partner gets a nice foot rub out of the deal.

"I Treasure You" Chest

Get a small recipe card box. Decorate and personalize it for your spouse. Inside place a single index card that says something like, "This is an 'I Treasure You Chest' where you can store your 'treasure cards.' Each card tells how much I treasure you." Then, every so often leave an index card somewhere where your sweetie will find it. On the card write a little something. It could be the line from a song, a thank you for something your sweetie did, a verse from the Bible (see page 47), a quote on love, a line from a movie or just your own special thought.

One fun idea is to spread a poem over several cards and hide them so they are found over a week or two. As you come up with other ideas, make some cards serious and some cards funny. Your partner can place all the collected cards in the "I Treasure You" Chest and can read over them whenever they feel a need for a boost. For a nice addition, you can get small stickers that say "I Love You" or are in the shape of a heart. Place a sticker on each card before hiding or delivering it.

Fortune Cookie Game

Prepare a a bunch of small, fortune cookie size, strips of paper with sayings like:

- Tell what you find most attractive about your sweetie
- Express gratitude for something your sweetie has done
- If you could go on a vacation anywhere, where would it be?
- You are going to be stranded an island together, what would you take?

Be creative. The "fortunes" should be about hopes, dreams and aspirations. Also they need to include suggestions on giving a compliment and also to remember shared moments together.

Then, for each "fortune," take a fortune cookie and wrap it in a damp paper towel and microwave for 30 seconds. Quickly and carefully open the softened cookie, remove the original fortune and replace it with your own fortune. Reshape and hold the cookie until it gets hard again.

Now spend some time together as a couple taking turns opening the fortune cookies and doing as the fortune directs. This can be a lot of fun for just the two of you or for the whole family.

Tell Her About It

People forget. Emotionally, everyone lives in the present. The past is gone and cannot be changed. The future is a long way off. The only real existence, emotionaly-speaking, is now. Keep this in mind while considering romance with your sweetie.

Billy Joel sings a song called "Tell Her About It." Usually one would not seek advice from pop music on relationships, unless it is bad advice one seeks. Never the less, the theme of this song goes right to the point. Even if you have told your sweetie many, many times that you love them, they still need to hear it again and often. Emotionally we think "Sure, you said you loved me yesterday, but what about today?" Is it logical? No. Does it make sense? No.

Unless you remember that emotions don't deal with the past very well. Its the higher areas of reasoning that understand the more abstract concepts of time.

But, emotions tend to overrule reason. So even though your sweetie "knows" you love her, she might not "feel" loved at the moment. Feeling almost always takes precedence over knowing.

Help your wife or husband know you love them by letting them feel loved by you. In other words, "Tell Her About It."

It's the Thought that Counts

In this book (and many others) you will see many wonderful ideas for expressing love and gratitude to your sweetie. Among all these ideas is a common thread: go one step beyond the normal. Instead of saying the word, "I love you," write it in a note. Instead of just saying "thank you," send a thank-you singing telegram.

Why bother? A couple of reasons. First, when you do something outside the ordinary and unexpected, you place yourself at a certain amount of emotional risk. Your sweetie will sense this. This moves you both outside of your combined comfort zone and adds excitement to the relationship. The comfort zone is comfortable but boring. By moving both of you outside of that boring place, a simple yet extra-ordinary act is a simple way of adding excitement to the relationship.

Second, as the saying goes, "it is the thought that counts." The more thought and preparation you put into sending your message of love and gratitude, the more it will count. As another saying states, "talk is cheap." You can say "I love you" over and over again. Yet it's impact is not very great. Speaking the words requires little effort and no thought. Sending a small card with a short hand-written note shows both thought and preparation. It is a small amount of effort, but it shows you are thinking of your sweetie, even when you are not together.

Third, do not spend a lot of money. There is a paradox of affluence. We are told that buying luxurious gifts will make our sweetie happy. However, you can't buy the affection of your sweetheart. Instead, save your money and give a bit of your time and talents instead.

Treasure Box

During the years of a couple's marriage, they gather momentos. These little tokens of particularly special times in our lives don't cost a lot. However, they can mean a lot to a couple because of the memories associated with them. Life is busy and these little things can get lost or overlooked.

Get yourself a box for these little treasures. Make it a nice box, like a jewelry box. Put all your special trinkets in the box. Then on your anniversary, open the box and share those moments again. Make a point of adding something new to the box at least once a year.

Comfort an Ailing Sweetie

My sweetie had been under the weather. Being the gallant husband I am, it is difficult to not be able to don my shiny armor and ride to her rescue on my snowy white steed. Many times during our marriage I have felt helpless because there is nothing I can do to "make it all better." No matter how many dragons I might slay, my sweetie is still going to suffer from a cold.

I have learned that just because you can't fix it all, doesn't mean you can't do something. This time that something was buying a dozens roses that were on sale at the store and renting a movie. Even though I can't make it better, I can remind her I am thinking of her and her needs.

The Danger of a Grand Gesture

Maybe it is just a guy thing, but I love to give my sweetie extravagant gifts. I hark back to the caveman days when bringing home a squirrel would keep your family from starving but not much else. However, a woolly mammoth will keep your wife and kids well fed and warm for quite a while. Also, it is an ego boost to have my wife show off my latest purchase.

Come to think of it, its not just a guy thing. My wife loves to lavish me with expensive gifts and toys. Maybe its just that we get such enjoyment out of seeing our sweetheart happy. And obviously the more money I spend the happier they will be. Right?

I have learned to keep these Neanderthal impulses under control. Buying an expensive gift can do more harm to your romantic life than it does good. Often, a small, but thoughtful token of love is better than an expensive one. Seems counter-intuitive so lets explore.

First, take into account the family budget. If you spend so much on a gift that it adversely affects the cash flow situation, the grand gesture is going to backfire. When your sweetie sees or thinks about the budget-busting gift, they will not be happy and grateful. Rather, your spouse will feel guilty and ashamed. This is not what you wanted. For long-term happiness, avoid the budget-buster. Remember this wise saying: There is no better aphrodisiac than a balanced budget.

Second, consider the idea of "points." When you do something nice for your sweetie, you are said to have scored points with them. Now the weird thing is that points are not proportional to money spent.

Consider the story of a wise friend of mine. He got his wife a new car. He also got her wedding ring upgraded for their anniversary. A foolish man would think that he would have scored enough points to last a long time. He would think "I spent so much money she is going to be happy and I won't have to worry about any of that romantic stuff for a long time." My wise friend realized that these points would only last a few days. Once she had shown all her friends and family the car, it would go back to being just a car. The same applies for the ring.

Which leads us to emotional memory. Our emotions have no memory. Emotions only exist in the **now** . It doesn't really matter how I felt last week, last year or five minutes ago. What matters is what I feel *now*. So the joy that your sweetie feels with the gift only lasts for a short time, regardless of the size and price of the gift. Some gifts can bring repeated joy to the recipient, but that is a topic for another day.

The bottom line is: You can score more points with small romatic gestures randomly strewn throughtout the year than with a single grand gesture. Emotions are fleeting—what was exciting yesterday becomes routine and boring today. Do unexpected, simple, and inexpensive gestures often to remind your sweetie how much you still love each other.

A Little Shoulder Rub

Next time your husband is facing away from you, sneak up and start rubbing his shoulders. It great for both the mind and the body. I am sure the wives wouldn't mind a nice shoulder rub either.

The Magic Pill

An aphrodisiac is a mythically magic pill that will put the fire back into a re-altionship. Although many things are rumored to have this effect, the most effective aphrodisiac is to remove all the anti-aphrodisiacs in the relationship. A big anti-aphrodisiac is boredom. As a marriage progresses, it naturally finds a routine. It is then easy to move from the routine to the taking each other for granted. Both those tendencies combine together to create boredom and a feeling that you are not appreciated.

To avoid boredom, do something to break the routine and express gratitude at the same time. Surprise your spouse and let her know how grateful you are for her. Try holding hands (see page 3) for a start. Is a single romantic gesture going to be a magic pill? Probably not. But what comes close to the magic pill is generating a sense of closeness and appreciation with your sweetie by not allowing her to feel that she is being taken for granted.

Remembering Romantic Gestures

Take a moment and thank you sweetie for some romantic gesture you really ap-preciated. Do not couch it as a "you used to do nice things but don't anymore." Instead, just thank him with something like "it was so much fun when...." This will do two things. First, it will let you both share the moment again. Second, it encourages your sweetie to do romantic things by showing that you remember and appreciate it long after the fact.

Falling In Love Many Times

I came across this quote from Mignon McLaughlin on the Quote of the Day[1] page:

> A successful marriage requires falling in love many times, always with the same person.

Through the course of our marriage, both of us have grown and changed. Things we once thought were important now seem so trivial. While things we once overlooked or never really considered have become central to our lives. How can we keep in touch with each other as we both change?

Dating. Isn't that how you first fell in love? Dating, is as important, if not more important, to married couples as it is to single people. Dating is how you got to know your partner in the first place. Dating is how you can continue to get to know your sweetheart as you both change over the years. Take time to get to know that incredible person you married. Take time to do it over and over again. Chances are your sweetheart is pretty wonderful.

Laugh a Little

Share a laugh with your sweetie. Need a laugh to share? Here are some reliable sources of humor:

- That guy at work who is always doing funny things
- The humor section of a magazine (think *Reader's Digest*, "Laughter is the best medicine")
- Recall a silly thing that happened on your honeymoon
- The kids are almost always good for a laugh
- If you don't have any, there are other peoples jokes[2]

---

[1] http://www.quotationspage.com/qotd.html
[2] http://m0smith.freeshell.org/blog-humor/blogger.html

Get Sweaty Regularly

The article on swimming (see page 121) mentions that exercise is good for a couple. In this article we'll delve into that idea.

When we exercise, we create endorphins in the brain. Endorphins have many benefits[1] including:

- More constructive responses to disappointments and failures
- Decreased feelings of stress and tension
- Increased perceptions of acceptance by others

Add these things up and what do you get? A great way for you and your sweetheart to spend some time together. The endorphins make you feel better about yourself. Then they will make you feel more accepted by your sweetie. Your sweetie, on the other hand will be feeling the same way. You will both feel better about yourself and your sweetheart.

Wait, it gets better. The feelings of stress are diminished while your ability to deal with stress is improved. Also, your problem solving abilities are improved as well. Marriage and family are stressful. There are a lot of demands on our time and energies. By exercising regularly, you won't reduce those demands, but you will increase your ability to cope with them. The net result is that you will be a better sweetie for your sweetheart.

By setting up a regular exercise date with your sweetie, you can get all these benefits and more. Not to mention all the health benefits of exercise. There is very little you could do that would improve the closeness of your relationship more than exercise. Break a sweat together.

Turn Off the TV & Step Away From the Remote

Have you ever met someone who dominated every conversation? Do you know a person who has the gift of being able to talk for extended periods of time without taking a breath? How do you feel after trying to hold a conversation with a person who keeps changing the subject? What about one who interrupts

---

[1] http://studenthealth.oregonstate.edu/topics/exercise-stress.php

other people's conversations? It can be a very frustrating experience trying to talk to a person who doesn't listen and won't allow other people to converse without interjecting.

Surprisingly, most of us invite such a one into our home everyday. Who is it? It is the television. The television talks non-stop all day long, is great at capturing one's attention and refuses to listen to anything anyone says to it.

Many times my sweetie and I will be talking and one of us will be distracted by the television. At that point a couple of things happen. If it was the person speaking, they will lose their train of thought and become frustrated. If the listener is distracted, the speaker feels bad that watching the television is more important than listening to what is being said.

Today's tip is to not have the TV on so much. Turn it off, especially when your spouse is trying to speak with you. You will enjoy the conversation much more. Don't make a big show of turning off the television because your sweetie might feel like they are intruding. Even better, leave it off when you are expecting your sweetheart so you can give her your undivided attention.

The kids are much more cooperative when the TV goes off. Its almost like a switch is thrown in their brains. Its an amazing thing to watch.

Communication is the life blood of a relationship. Anything that hampers the flow of communication dampens the relationship. Let the communication flow freely by removing ditractions.

Keeping Special Things Special

For special occasions my wife sometimes gets breakfast in bed. This happens maybe twice a year for Valentine's Day and for her birthday. She really likes the attention and the kids enjoying helping in the surprise. Since it only happens once or twice a year it can be a real treat.

What would happen if she got breakfast in bed everyday? It would stop being special. It would become commonplace and maybe even boring. Soon she would come to expect it and feel disappointed when it didn't happen.

You and your sweetie share some special events and occasions. Keep them special by keeping them rare. That way you ensure that the special things stay special.

A Kiss a Day

I found this floating around the internet:

> Studies indicate that a man who kisses his wife good-bye when he leaves for work every morning averages a higher income than those who don't. Husbands who exercise the rituals of affection tend to be more painstaking, more stable, more methodical, thus, higher earners. Studies also show that men who kiss their wives before leaving in the morning live five years longer than those who don't.

Isn't that amazing? It seems that just by kissing your wife you can make more money and live longer. However, I could not find the actual study that shows this relationship between kissing and money. Remember that anything found on the internet must be checked[1].

Even if it does not raise your income or make you live longer, kissing your sweetie in the morning is a great habit to have. Since you are going to be apart from your sweetheart for most of the waking day, make sure that the thing that happens last before you part company is a sign of affection. Pair that goodbye kiss with a welcome home kiss at the end of the day.

Let your kids see you kissing. They need to know that their parents love and care for each other.

No Strings Attached

Do something for your sweetie with "no strings attached." Let me give you an example of "strings attached." First, the wife cooks the husband's favorite dinner to butter him up so she can ask him to take her shopping. Or, the husband gets very helpful with the chores so the wife will feel better about him going out with the guys. Admittedly, these are stereotypical examples but they help to illustrate the point that we often try to manipulate our spouse by doing things for them so they will do something for us. When we do things this way, what happens?

---

[1] http://www.snopes.com/

- Your sweetheart feels manipulated. She/he will begin to start asking, "What is it now?" every time you try and do something nice for them.
- You will feel that your sweetie owes you the thing you want. If she/he doesn't give you what you want you will feel cheated.
- It works to douse the romantic flame of the marriage.

Now, consider doing something special without any expectation in return. Help with the chores just to be helpful. Cook his favorite meal, just because he likes it.

Don't forget to smile (see page 1) to show you really love your sweetheart, even if you don't enjoy the task.

Laughing is Also Good For You

For years we have heard that laughter is the best medicine[1]. I even wrote about laughing in a previous article entitled "Laugh a Little" (see page 10) . Now there is some research on why laughter is good for you. An article, *Laughter May Be Good for the Heart, Study Finds*, in the news states:

> A daily dose of laughter may be good for the heart because, like exercise, it makes blood vessels work more efficiently, U.S. researchers reported.

While not a replacement for exercise, laughter it seems, really does have some physical benefits to it. Of course more research needs to be done in this area, but the conclusion of the study is still interesting. The study only included twenty participants so drawing any real conclusions at this time is premature. Yet, it does serve to remind us to laugh together as a couple and a family. Not a funny person? Need somewhere to find funny anecdotes? One of my favorites is Reader's Digest. Each issue has a lot of humorous family friendly stories. They have also published some of the best of the stories in book form. Of course there are lots of Joke of the Day[2] websites too. Laugh together often.

---

[1] http://m0smith.freeshell.org/blog-humor/blogger.html
[2] http://m0smith.freeshell.org/blog-humor/blogger.html

Passion

Do you have a passion?[1] in life? Passion, like most English words, has several meanings. When you are passionate about your sweetheart, it could mean *ardent love*. People can also be passionate about other things. In this sense, passion can mean *boundless enthusiasm* and that is the meaning for we'll address here.

What are some of the things you are passionate about? My passions include family history,[2] my wife and offspring, physical fitness, chess[3], improving my marriage, Toastmasters[4] and computer programming[5]. These are the things I like to do, enjoy doing and choose to do when I have some spare time. These articles, my blog and this book are part of my passion in making my marriage great.

What does all this have to do with romance in your marriage? Just this: sometimes in marriage we abandon the things we are passionate (boundless enthusiam) about in favor of passion (ardent love). For a healthy relationship, each partner needs to develop their individual interests and talents. Also, each needs to wholeheartedly support the other. This does not mean you have to enjoy your sweetie's hobbies, just that you make sure they have your support in pursuing them.

Take time for your interests, passions and hobbies. Ensure that your partner has time to develop personal interests and hobbies as well. Part of a healthy relationship is growth, as individuals as well as a couple. Change is an important part of growth, so remember to fall in love (see page 10), over and over as you each improve your talents and pursue your passions.

---

[1] http://www.answer.com/passion
[2] http://www.topoged.com/
[3] http://m0smith.freeshell.org/blog-chess/blogger.html
[4] http://www.toastmasters.org/
[5] http://m0smith.freeshell.org/2004/10/magic-triangle-java-program.html

"Does This Make Me Look Fat?"

Guys, has this ever happened to you? You are getting ready to go to a social engagement. You're all ready, the wife is looking good and putting the finishing touches on. Then, out of the blue, it happens:

Does this make me look fat?

The novice husband will answer either yes or no. Sounds like a "yes or no" type question, so it makes sense to answer with either answer. The novice husband then gains experience, but is left wondering why she is upset.

The more experienced husband realizes that neither yes nor no is the correct answer, but wonders what it might be. A primordial grunt usually suffices to keep one out of hot water. In a later posting, we'll revisit this subject on why yes and no are both wrong.

Ok, what is the answer to the question? The answer is to not answer the question. Let me explain. When your sweetie asks "does this make me look fat?" or some other such loaded question, use a bit of redirection.

Stop, look her up and down. Tell her to turn around slowly one direction, then the other. Have her walk a few paces away and turn again. Undo one of her buttons and do it back up. Then have her turn around again. Have her lift her skit up and check out her slip. Make some adjustments to her hair. Have her move under the light so you can get a closer look. Keep this up for a couple of minutes, really making a show of inspecting how show looks.

Finally, walk up to her, look her in eye (see page 1) and say "YOU'RE GORGEOUS!"

Fixed Patterns

> All fixed set patterns are incapable of adaptability or pliability. The truth is outside of all fixed patterns.
>
> — Bruce Lee

As you probably know, Bruce Lee was a martial arts expert as well as a movie star. He even created his own form of martial arts.

In martial arts, patterns are fixed routines, similar to a choreographed dance routine. A pattern consists of a set of movements and is an important part of the study of martial arts. Part of receiving an advancement to the next belt rank involves mastery of a new pattern.

Bruce Lee recognized that, while patterns are important, they are only a tool. It would be foolish to expect to follow a pattern in a sparring match or a real fight and expect to win. Facing an opponent requires moving outside the pattern and reacting to the reality of the situation.

A marriage relationship has set patterns as well. Get up, go to work, come home, yard work, kids' homework, etc etc etc. Yet, as Bruce Lee noted, the truth is outside these patterns. Patterns, while important, become boring. Make time to move outside the patterns of life and into the romance. It is in the exceptional, the extraordinary and the unexpected where romance is to be found.

Peppermint for the Tootsies

A couple of previous articles, *How About a Foot Rub* (see page 4) and *Sweetie Appreciation Week* (see page 107) talked about how wonderful it can be to get a foot rub. My wife is particularly fond of them.

One way to improve a foot rub is to use peppermint foot lotion. It feels great and soothing without making your sweetie's feet cold.

Tip: When applying lotion, put some on your hands and rub them together. This will warm up both the lotion and your hands, making the foot rub much more enjoyable.

Eight Gifts That Don't Cost a Cent

I found the following floating around the internet and it is worth sharing exactly as it is. Thanks to *Anonymous* who wrote it:

The Gift of Listening

But you must really listen. Don't interrupt, don't daydream, don' t plan your response. Just listen.

The Gift of Affection

Be generous with appropriate hugs, kisses, pats on the back and handholds. Let these small actions demonstrate the love you have for family and friends.

The Gift of Laughter

Clip cartoons. Share articles and funny stories. Your gift will say, "I love to laugh with you."

The Gift of Solitude

There are times when we want nothing better than to be left alone. Be sensitive to those times and give the gift of solitude to others.

The Gift of a Favor

Everyday, go out of your way to do something kind.

The Gift of a Written Note

It can be a simple "thanks for the help" note or a full sonnet. A brief, handwritten note may be remembered for a lifetime.

The Gift of a Compliment

A simple and sincere, "you look great in red," "you did a super job," or "that was a wonderful meal" can make someone's day.

The Gift of a Cheerful Disposition

The easiest way to feel good is to extend a kind word to someone.

Work to give your sweetie at least one of these gifts every day.

Paying Compliments

Many people do not know how to take a sincere compliment. Part of the problem may be that people do not receive compliments often (see page 5) enough to have practice gracefully accept them. Also, since they are rare, we wonder what it is the person wants from us. Is this really a compliment or am I just being buttered up? People also fear that accepting a compliment appears arrogant.

What do people do when they receive a compliment? A common response is to put yourself down. Consider this common exchange:

"You have a wonderful singing voice."
"I was off key."

What follows is that the giver of the compliment feels the need to reinforce the compliment while the receiver feels the need to continue to put themselves down with each compliment so as to appear modest. The net result can be that both parties feel poorly with the exchange.

How to receive a compliment

Simply say: "Thank you, that was very kind of you to say."

Notice how the receiver does not appear immodest because they are thanking them for the nice words they said. The giver feels as though the compliment was accepted. This response also works if you are just being buttered up because it does not increase your own sense of self-importance.

How to give a compliment.

Give it in a way that allows for no argument. One way is to write it in a note (see page 2). You can't argue with a note so there is no need for the receiver to defend their sense of modesty. Notes also work because they seem more sincere.

When I was looking for a birthday card the other day, I ran across some cards I hadn't noticed before. As you know, the greeting cards are divided into categories like Birthday, Mother's Day, Graduation, etc. There is a section I hadn't really paid attention to called Encouragement. As I read through the cards, I discovered that the thoughts contained within these cards were the kind of things I wanted my wife to know, but that she would feel the need to put herself down if I were to say them.

Next time you want to pay your sweetheart a compliment, consider taking the time (see page 6) to find a nice card and writing your thoughts. It will make your compliment that much more appreciated because of the time and effort spent in preparing it.

Johnny Lingo's Eight Cow Wife

There is a story of Johnny Lingo which you can read[1] and has been made into a short film[2]. The story is one of a Polynesian trader who goes bargaining for a wife. No one can understand when he offers the unheard of sum of eight cows for a girl that most consider not worth even two cows. Johnny, it turns out, is a good trader after all.

---

[1] http://www.biblehelp.org/cow.htm
[2] http://www.ldscatalog.com/

People live up to or down to others expectations (see page 50) of them. Tell a kid they are stupid and they will believe it for the rest of their life. Treat a kid as if they are intelligent and they perform better in school. As quoted in ERIC Digest 116 July 1997[1] on expectations for students:

> Students tend to internalize the beliefs teachers have about their ability. Generally, they "rise or fall to the level of expectation of their teachers.... When teachers believe in students, students believe in themselves. When those you respect think you can, you think you can."

Living to expectation applies not just to students, but to your spouse as well. Criticism, labels, names and other put downs will start to be internalized by your companion. Compliments, praise and other expressions of approval will also be internalized and reflected by your sweetheart.

The lesson of Johnny Lingo is that if you want to have the best spouse on the planet, treat your spouse as if he was already the best.

Whistle While You Work

Do you like doing chores? Do you enjoy going to work? Do you look forward to all those things you hate to do? Whether you like it or not, there are certain things you have to do that you do not like to do. It might be dishes, laundry, yard work or just work work.

A previous article discussed having passion (see page 15) for some things in your life. Today, we are not talking about those things, but the things we don't really want to do. As parents and adults, there are some things that just have to be done. As responsible adults we have to make sure they happen.

What is our attitude about these chores? Do we gripe about chores? Do we complain about work? Do we find ways to put it off, so we can complain and gripe about it more? Do we spend more time complaining than it would take to do the chore?

What has this to do with romance and flirting? Chores and work are about as far from romance and flirting as you can get. The answer is enthusiasm. There is something about an enthusiastic person that makes everyone around them feel alive. We want to be around enthusiastic people, we are attracted to enthusiastic people. Enthusiasm is contagious and we all want to catch it. Of

---

[1] http://eric.uoregon.edu/publications/digests/digest116.html

course, complaining and griping are about as unenthusiastic as you can get. And if people like to be around enthusiastic people . . . Well, you get the idea.

So, repeat after me "Yippee! I get to do dishes today." No, sarcasm is not enthusiasm. Ok, so you don't have to like doing the dishes to be enthusiastic while doing the dishes. Just whistle while you work. Maybe put on some music you like and dance around while doing the dishes. Sing or whistle. The trick is: don't be disagreeable just because you are doing a disagreeable task.

Remember to take time to smile (see page 1). The more enthusiastic you are about life in general, the more your partner will want to be around you. The more *joie de vivre* you have, the better your kids will respond. The more enthusiastic you are, the more enthusiastic other people will be about you, especially your sweetie.

To Teach, To Learn

I received feedback about one couple who had enjoyed time working on the car together. Every person has things they are good at and are knowledgeable about. Likewise, every person has things they do not understand and really do not do very well.

There is something about teaching that makes one feel good. Its fun to watch as another person learns and grows. Learning is just as fun. Finding out you really can do what you thought you could not do, or were even afraid to try. Both the teacher and the student grow from the experience.

Think about yourself and your spouse. What are some things that they could teach you? Schedule a date and ask your sweetheart to help you learn.

- Simple auto maintenance
- Cooking your favorite meal
- Chess
- Golf

A note on being teachable: As adults we are used to being able to do everything well. It can be a really ego-struggle to admit that there are some things we are not good at and allow ourselves to be taught. You need to leave your ego at the door and really try to learn.

A note to teachers: Keep the above note in mind. Of course it would be easier to complete the task yourself. Be patient.

Bragging Rights

In the movie, Johnny Lingo (see page 19), Johnny tells that when the women gather and talk, they discuss about how many cows their husband bargained for them. The one whose husband saw fit to give her father the most cows had the bragging rights. In real life, people like to play this same game of one-upsmanship. We all like to stand out and we all like to have a story to tell. There is something about human nature and group dynamics that makes us want to be part of the group and stand out in the crowd at the same time.

Here's an example. I have noticed that when my wife gets together with other women the talk will sometimes turn to wedding rings, especially if there is a newly engaged girl in the group. Each woman will have some story to tell that makes their ring unique. One diamond is so big. Another has a special cut to it. The crown on this ring is made of stronger stuff. My wife's stone isn't the biggest, but she designed the ring and had it custom created by a friend. While each woman is part of the group, each has a unique story to share that is individual to them. If one of the women doesn't have something unique to tell about her ring, she feels left out to a certain extent.

This is not just a girl thing either. The guys do it as well. Next chance you get, listen to guys talk about computers, cars, trucks, power tools, etc. We all love having a story to tell that others find interesting.

Give your sweetie something to brag about. Provide a story that will be interesting to tell in small groups where people like to swap stories. No, the fact that you scored 12,763,470 points in Pac-man is not something your sweetie will be able to brag about, unless the conversation drifts into "the doofus things my husband has done." One area to have bragging rights is in romantic gestures, keeping in mind not to go overboard (see page 7), here some ideas of things you can do to give your sweetheart those important bragging rights:

- Create your own holiday (see page 61)
- Send a bouquet or singing telegram to work
- Ambush Getaway (see page 59)
- When you sweetie needs help, do more than is expected (see page 51)
- Burma Shave (see page 106) signs
- Treat your sweetie like a VIP (see page 62) for an evening

That will do to start with. Also, remember that you have talents unique to you. Sharing and exploring those talents can also be the stuff of good tales. While scoring a bazillion points on a video game is not what we want, winning a game tournament is.... ok its still doofus. But competing and doing well are always good for stories and bragging rights. Even competing and not doing well is still better than not having tried at all.

The following are a few specific examples, but you have your own talents and will need to adapt these ideas to your own situation. The important idea is to get outside the comfort zone with your talents and share them more publicly than you have done:

- If your talent is photography, enter a picture of him/her in the county or state fair
- If your talent is singing, publically serenade them

"Does This Make Me Look Fat?" Part II

Previously, how to answer the dreaded question " Does this make me look fat?" (see page 16) was discussed. Why do people ask these sorts of questions, knowing full well that any answer is the wrong answer?

First, this is not just a girl thing. Guys ask these same sorts of questions as well. I find myself asking my wife, "Hey sweetie, what do you think of this thing I did?" The last thing I really want is for her to tell me what she thinks. Just as the last thing she really wants to hear from me is if she is fat.

What we both really want is assurance. For some reason the asker has a feeling of self-doubt and needs to be assured. Consider the situation where a woman is going to a ten year high school reunion. There will be people there she has not seen in many years and she wants to make a good impression. She is worried about how she looks, what her classmates will think of her and she wants to look her best. This situation can cause even the most confident person to question themselves.

Situations arise once in a while where we step outside our comfort zone. The further outside the zone we get, the less sure we are of ourselves. The comfort zone is where we feel in control, where life is ordered, and where we have experience. Outside the comfort zone life is not in our control. Fear and insecurity live outside the comfort zone. People who stray far outside their comfort zone need assuring that they will still be ok.

But, people never say "I need assuring." Sure your spouse will say nice things about you, but there is the question of how genuine the feelings are. Are these nice things true or just what I wanted to hear? Instead, we go fishing for assurances. We ask a question like "does this make me look fat?" That way we feel more certain of the sincerity of the answer.

That also explains why neither "yes" nor "no" works very well as an answer. Neither answer provides the assurance the asker is needing. When your spouse asks you a seemingly impossible question, check the context in which the question is being asked. Has your sweetheart left their comfort zone and done something new or different? When your spouse is planning on leaving the comfort zone , she will need encouragement. Answer the question in such as way as to give assurance. Your companion will really appreciate it.

Complementing Each Other

In My Fair Lady, Professor Henry Higgins wonders, "why can't a woman be more like a man?" I don't think he is the only man to ask that question. Neither is it just a guy thing—woman wonder why men aren't more like them as well. After all, we like to be with people like us.

Today we are going talk about complementing your sweetie, not complimenting (see page 18). The dictionary says that complement[1] means:

> Either of two parts that complete the whole or mutually complete each other.

Think of it as two puzzle pieces that fit together. The pieces are not the same shape, yet together they form a complete picture. The same thing applies with married couples.

Gordon B. Hinckley once said:

> In His grand design, when God first created man, He created a duality of the sexes. The ennobling expression of that duality is found in marriage. One individual is complementary to the other.

He then went on to quote in 1 Corinthians how neither the man is without the woman and the woman without the man (see page 51). A marriage is not the

---

[1] http://www.answers.com/complement&r=67

pairing of likes, nor is it the welding of opposites. Instead, it is the union of the elements which come together to complete each other.

Getting Dressed Up

I used to work at a job that required a lot of travel. I would be gone two weeks at a time and come home on Friday. Then on Monday there was another flight out again. On occasion I had to be gone even longer than two weeks. Spending that much time apart can be very trying on the marriage and on the kids, as you can imagine. My sweetie is a real trooper and supported me in all this traveling, even when it was so hard for her to effectively be a single parent.

For some reason women quit wearing makeup after being married for a while. The husbands don't seem to mind all that much. After all, you married your gal, not Mary Kay or Revlon. Makeup becomes a special occasion thing. My wife uses it when she wants to look extra nice or for that special evening out on the town.

Once, when I had been on the road for quite a while, we had planned to go out and spend the evening with some people the evening I got home. She greeted me in the usual way. That evening, my sweetie spent quite a bit of time getting ready for the evening; getting her hair just right, putting on makeup and wearing some of her "going out" clothes. She looked really nice and we had a good time. However, I felt a little bad that she was so concerned about looking good for our friends, when I had been gone for so long. It was silly to be jealous, but emotions are often silly that way.

For the gals: Remember to make going out or spending time with your hubby a special occasion as well. Take the time to get dressed up for your spouse every now and again, just as you would an '"important" person you were going to spend the evening with. Just cause this guy loves you doesn't mean you shouldn't make him say "wow" every now and again, like when you were dating.

For the guys: Give your sweetie reasons to get "dressed up." Take her out to more formal places so she will want to look her best. Also, do your best to look your best. Dress nice for her. Gals like being out with a sharply dressed man.

A Travel Reminder

Does your sweetie really like your cologne or perfume? Did you know that the sense of smell is strongly associated with memories? Sometimes I am walking down the street and out of the blue a certain smell will trigger some long forgotten memories and their associated emotions. Smell can be a very powerful trigger.

If you are traveling without your partner, take along your cologne or perfume. Send a love letter and put a few drops on the papers. Be sure to include SWAK on the outside of the envelope. The familiar fragrance will be a nice surprise.

If your sweetie is traveling without you, sneak a small hankie or stuffed animal into your sweetheart's luggage. Put a few drops of perfume or cologne on it. Make sure it is sealed in a baggie or something so their entire luggage doesn't smell. It will make a nice surprise when they are missing you.

Loose Lips Sink Ships

Every so often we hear the phrase *loose lips sink ships*. The phrase was used as the name of a poster campaign during World War II to emphasize national security. The message was that idle talk could endanger the soldiers fighting in the war. Of course, both sides were trying to gather information in order the defeat the other. Since you never really know who might hear a conversation, it was safer not to talk about anything to do with the military.

Of course, the basic problem was one of trust. Maybe you trust your friend, but not the person overhearing the conversation. Besides, some people just don't know how to keep secrets either. They mean no harm but don't stop to look at the consequences of their idle talk.

In a marriage, trust is vitally important. Both partners need to feel that they can share deeply personal feelings, ideas and problems with each other. Likewise, your spouse should trust you to listen as well. It is so important to hold these confidences between just the husband and wife. Just as loose talk can sink a ship, so can loose talk strain a marriage.

It can be very hurtful to have a confidence betrayed. Let your sweetheart know how much he means to you by not sharing the intimate details of your life together.

Communication and Marriage

James E Faust stated:

> Marriage relationships can be enriched by better communication. One important way is to pray together. This will resolve many of the differences, if there are any, between the couple before sleep comes. I do not mean to overemphasize differences, but they are real, and make things interesting. Our differences are the little pinches of salt which can make the marriage seem sweeter. We communicate in a thousand ways, such as a smile, a brush of the hair, a gentle touch, and remembering each day to say "I love you" and the husband to say "You're beautiful." Some other important words to say, when appropriate, are "I'm sorry." Listening is excellent communication.

So many great ideas in a single paragraph.

Prayer

Praying with each other and for each other is a powerful influence for good in a marriage and in a family. Imagine how your spouse feels hearing you thank God daily for them and your relationship. Praying invites peace and harmony into the home. It is the basis for the inspiration that is needed when raising children and overcoming the difficulties that arise in a relationship. Pray daily and thank God for your spouse.

Non-verbal communication

We often think of communication as verbal: speaking and listening. Yet a lot of communication happens through the other senses. We see a smile and feel a gentle touch, a soft stroke or a pat on the back. While verbal communication is important, non-verbal communication is also important and can be much more effective. Saying "I love you" is important, but smiling and holding hands while saying it makes it that much more meaningful. Remember the importance of non-verbal communication and go give your husband or wife a big bear hug.

Compliments

For some reason, people tend to focus on the negative and ignore the positive. Be sure to focus on the positive with your spouse. Compliment your companion on their looks, on a job well done and on being such a wonderful spouse and parent. To make the compliment more meaningful, write it down. Spoken words are ethereal. Once spoken they are gone, never to be retrieved again. The written word adds permanence and reality. Writing thoughts makes them more real because they can be seen, touched and read over and over again. Write your sweetie a compliment today.

Listening

Make time for talking and listening. Listening is more than hearing. It's really paying attention. Its turning off the TV and removing other distractions. Its stopping what you are doing so you can dedicate your whole attention to to the conversation. Listening shows your love by deomstrating how important your spouse's ideas and concerns are to you. Make time to talk and and take time to listen.

The Greatest Joy

I saw this quote the other day: "Our greatest joy and satisfaction comes from the act of giving. — Leo Buscaglia." If you would be happy in your relationship with your sweetie, practice the act of giving. The more selfless you are, the more you will get out of the marriage. The more selfish you are, the less the meaningful the relationship will be.

Opening the Door

Previously I wrote about needing to do the simple courtesies liking holding doors opens. Yesterday I surprised my sweetie by actually going around and opening the door of the car for her. We had been visiting her sister's and were leaving. The rest of the family was in the vehicle and my sweetheart had stopped on the porch to say good-bye. As my wife started to walk toward the car I realized it was a great opportunity to show her a simple courtesy. So I jumped out of the car, and walked over toward her door. My wife asked "What's the matter?" I said nothing, just smiled and opened the door for her. She just beamed.

I learned a couple of things. First, its been a lot longer than I thought since I had shown my sweetheart that simple courtesy. I was a bit surprised when she thought something was wrong, but it has been a while since I opened the door for her. Second, a small amount of extra effort goes a long way. Small and simple acts of kindness are the fuel that keeps the fire alive.

Combine Your Hearts into One

Shakespeare, speaking in Henry the Fifth, said, "God, the best maker of all marriages, combine your hearts in one" (*Henry* V, act 5, scene 2). Be unified in all you do. This does not mean to do everything together, but truly and wholehearted support each other in all that you do.

Grow Your Love to Mighty Proportions

Total unselfishness is sure to accomplish another factor in successful marriage. If one is forever seeking the interests, comforts, and happiness of the other, the love found in courtship and cemented in marriage will grow into mighty proportions. Many couples permit their marriages to become stale and their love to grow cold like old bread or worn-out jokes or cold gravy. Certainly the foods most vital for love are consideration, kindness, thoughtfulness, concern, expressions of affection, embraces of appreciation, admiration, pride, companionship, confidence, faith, partnership, equality, and interdependence.

— Spencer W. Kimball

There is a profound paradox to be found in a successful marriage. Rather than focus on what I need, I need to focus on the needs of my companion. Only by focusing on the needs of my eternal companion can my needs truly be met.

The Good Wife's Guide

My friend forwarded me an email making the rounds. The subject line was "The Good Wife's Guide" and it appears to be making the rounds on the internet. I liked it so much I included it on my Humor website[▶].

It is supposed to be from a 1955 "Housekeeping Magazine" and I have not checked whether it is a fake or if it was real. Regardless, it is funny. My wife had a good laugh over it.

While the none of the items on the list itself is not going to be taken very seriously, there is one grain of value that can be gleaned. It is the essence behind several of the suggestions. The thing we can apply is the notion of "preparing to greet your spouse."

Think about it. My wife and I spend most of our time apart. Those first few moments when we meet in the evening seem to be most critical. If we greet each other warmly and with a smile, it sets a cheerful tone for the rest of the evening. If, contrariwise, we are grumpy and grouchy, the whole evening gets off on the wrong foot.

Bottom line: before coming home or when your spouse arrives, greet him with a smile and a hug. Let your sweetie know that you are glad to be together again. Spending a few moments enjoying each other's company will go a long way toward making the rest of the evening a pleasant one.

Imagine the impact it will have on the kids if they see how important their parents' relationship is to them. With all the bad examples of marriages that we are barraged with, setting a good example of proper priorities is most important.

They Lived Happily Ever After

Many TV shows and fictional stories end with marriage: "They lived happily ever after." We have come to realize that the mere performance of a ceremony does not bring happiness and a successful marriage. Happiness does not come by pressing a button, as does the electric light; happiness is a state of mind and comes from within. It must be earned. It cannot be purchased with money; it cannot be taken for nothing.

Spencer W. Kimball once said, "Some think of happiness as a glamorous life of ease, luxury, and constant thrills; but true marriage is based on a happiness which is more than that, one which comes from giving, serving, sharing, sacrificing, and selflessness."

The honeymoon doesn't have to end, it just needs to adapt. By following the principles of giving, serving, sharing, sacrificing and selflessness, the feelings

---

[14] http://m0smith.freeshell.org/blog-humor/blogger.html

of love and joy can deepen over the years. Make the fire a bonfire rather than just smoldering embers. Just as a fire needs fuel to keep burning, so does a marriage. The fuel to keep the romance burning in your marriage is adhering to the above mentioned principles.

The Formula for a Successful Marriage Is Simple

"The formula [for a successful marriage] is simple; the ingredients are few, though there are many amplifications of each.

"First, there must be the proper approach toward marriage, which contemplates the selection of a spouse who reaches as nearly as possible the pinnacle of perfection in all the matters which are of importance to the individuals. And then those two parties must come to the altar in the temple realizing that they must work hard toward this successful joint living.

"Second, there must be a great unselfishness, forgetting self and directing all of the family life and all pertaining thereunto to the good of the family, subjugating self.

"Third, there must be continued courting and expressions of affection, kindness, and consideration to keep love alive and growing.

"Fourth, there must be a complete living of the commandments of the Lord as defined in the gospel of Jesus Christ.

"With these ingredients properly mixed and continually kept functioning, it is quite impossible for unhappiness to come, misunderstandings to continue, or breaks to occur. Divorce attorneys would need to transfer to other fields and divorce courts would be padlocked."

— Spencer W. Kimball

Always Assume the Best

I assume we have all heard the phrase "Don't assume. It makes an A** out of U and ME." I am going to take issue with that bit of wisdom . Have you ever looked assume[1] up in the dictionary? I have and it means lots of things, but the relevant definition is:

> To take for granted without proof; presuppose

---

[1] http://www.answers.com/assume&r=67

Language and communication being what they are, we are forced to take some things for granted when talking with anyone.

Let me use a classic miscommunication as an example. The guy says to a girl, "You look nice today." His intent was to pay her a sincere compliment. Often, at least in comedies, the girl will respond, "Oh! So you mean I don't look good every day?." What happened? How does a compliment become an insult?

It has to do with assumed intent. Does the guy intend to compliment the girl or has he really been disappointed with her looks and finally she looks nice, for once. The answer is that the girl, as listener has to decide. Of course, both guys and girls do this sort of verbal misinterpretation.

Whenever someone talks to us, we have to decide the intent of what is being said. We have a responsibility to decide. We have to assume, there is no choice. The problem arises when we assume incorrectly. When we assign the wrong intent to what is being said, the entire meaning will be changed; changing compliment to insutl. It is most important to understand the intent to comprehend the proper meaning of what is being said.

A great way to get the intent right is that when your spouse talks to you, always assume the best intent. Always put everything in the "best possible light." If your spouse really meant it that way, then your communication will be that much more enjoyable. Otherwise, you can often diffuse a tense situation and turn it into a comic misunderstanding in this way. Remember: The soft answer turneth away wrath.

Besides, your companion is a pretty great person. She was smart enough to marry you.

Points to Ponder

1. Anger is a condition in which the tongue, works faster than the mind.

2. You can't change the past, but you can ruin the present by worrying over the future.

3. Love . . . . .and you shall be loved.

4. God always gives His best to those who leave the choice with Him.

5. All people smile in the same language.

6. A hug is a great gift, one size fits all. It can be given for any occasion and it's easy to exchange.

7. Everyone needs to be loved, especially when they do not deserve it.

8. The real measure of a man's wealth is what he has invested in eternity.

9. Laughter is God's sunshine.

10. Everything has beauty but not everyone sees it.

11. It's important for parents to live the same things they teach.

12. Thank God for what you have, TRUST GOD for what you need.

13. If you fill your heart with regrets of yesterday and the worries of tomorrow, you have no today to be thankful for.

14. Happy memories never wear out.... Relive them as often as you want.

15. Home is the place where we grumble the most, but are often treated the best.

16. Man looks at outward appearance but the Lord looks within.

17. The choice you make today will usually affect tomorrow.

18. Take time to laugh for it is the music of the soul.

19. If anyone speaks badly of you, live so none will believe it.

20. Patience is the ability to idle your motor, when you feel like stripping your gears.

21. Love is strengthened by working through conflicts together.

22. The best thing parents can do for their children, is to love each other.

23. Harsh words break no bones but they do break hearts.

24. To get out of a difficulty, one usually must go through it.

25. We take for granted the things that we should be giving thanks for.

26. Love is the only thing that can be divided, without being diminished.

27. Happiness is enhanced by others but does not depend upon others.

28. You are richer today if you have laughed, given or forgiven.

29. For every minute you are angry with someone, you lose 60 seconds of happiness that you can never get back.

30. Do what you can, for who you can, with what you have, and where you are.

31. The best gifts to give: To your friend, loyalty; To your enemy, forgiveness; To your boss, service; To a child, a good example; To your parents, gratitude and devotion; To your mate, love and faithfulness; To all men and women, charity; and To God, your life.

Making the Best of Your Marriage

Nobody has things just as he would like them. The thing to do is to make a success with what material I have. It is a sheer waste of time and soul-power to imagine what I would do if things were different. They are not different.

Frank Crane

In a marriage, things are not always "perfect." Perfect is of course a relative idea. My idea of perfect and my sweetie's notion of perfection are not necessarily the same. We come from different backgrounds, with different life experiences and different expectations. Even after sixteen years of marriage, we still don't see through the same eyes.

How do we handle the differences? Do You pine away the time, wishing our sweetie were different, more perfect, more like yourself? Do you waste energy trying to perfect your sweetheart? Seems like a waste of time and energy.

It is far better to focus on the positive aspects of your spouse, your relationship and your life together. There are lots of wonderful things about your sweetie. Spend your time and effort in showing your appreciation for that fabulous person who married you. Expend some energy on finding unique ways of complimenting your sweetie more.

Rather than spending time and energy wishing things were different, spend that time and energy making things the best they can be.

Wisdom from Grandpa

I found these humorous[1] sayings floating about the Internet. They are both funny and thought provoking:

- If a man has enough horse sense to treat his wife like a thoroughbred, she will never turn into an old nag.
- On anniversaries, the wise husband always forgets the past—but never the present.
- A foolish husband says to his wife, "Honey, you stick to the washin', ironin', cookin' and scrubbin'. No wife of mine is gonna work."

Recipe for a Happy Family

I saw this recipe by Mrs. J. Alexander (in the *Keen Ager News*) and thought we needed to remember to cook up a happy family along with all the other Christmas and holiday cooking we do.

Ingredients:

- 1 Heartful of Love
- 1 Portion of Understanding
- 2 Handsful of Generosity
- 1 Dash of Faith

---

[1] http://m0smith.freeshell.org/blog-humor/blogger.html

- 1 Cup of Laughter
- 1 Heaping Tablespoon of Forgiveness

Directions:

Combine ingredients, and stir frequently with tenderness. Sprinkle freely with kindness and serve daily to your family.

Who Needs a Computer?

I saw this and laughed. Yes, my dear wife must remind me of my own siblings birthdays. I do manage to remember our anniversary every year all by myself though.

> Because I had forgotten the dates for a number of my friends' and relatives' birthdays and anniversaries, I decided to compile a list on the computer and have the dates highlighted on screen when the machine was turned on. I went to a number of computer stores to find a software program that would do the job but had no luck at the first few. I finally found one where the clerk seemed experienced.
>
> "Can you recommend something that will remind me of birthdays and anniversaries?" I asked. "Have you tried a wife?" he replied.

An Old Farmer's Advice

I saw this floating around the Internet:

- Your fences need to be horse-high, pig-tight and bull-strong.
- Keep skunks and bankers and lawyers at a distance.
- Life is simpler when you plow around the stump.
- A bumble bee is considerably faster than a John Deere tractor.
- Words that soak into your ears are whispered . . . not yelled.
- Meanness don't jes' happen overnight.
- Forgive your enemies. It messes up their heads.
- Do not corner something that you know is meaner than you.
- It don't take a very big person to carry a grudge.
- You cannot unsay a cruel word.
- Every path has a few puddles.

- When you wallow with pigs, expect to get dirty.
- The best sermons are lived, not preached.
- Most of the stuff people worry about ain't never gonna happen anyway.
- Don't judge folks by their relatives.
- Remember that silence is sometimes the best answer.
- Live a good, honorable life. Then when you get older and think back, you'll enjoy it a second time.
- Don't interfere with somethin' that ain't botherin' you none.
- Timing has a lot to do with the outcome of a rain dance.
- If you find yourself in a hole, the first thing to do is stop diggin'.
- Sometimes you get, and sometimes you get got.
- The biggest troublemaker you'll probably ever have to deal with, watches you from the mirror every mornin'.
- Always drink upstream from the herd.
- Good judgment comes from experience, and a lotta that comes from bad judgment.
- Lettin' the cat outta the bag is a whole lot easier than puttin' it back in.
- If you get to thinkin' you're a person of some influence, try orderin' somebody else's dog around.
- Live simply. Love generously. Care deeply. Speak kindly. Leave the rest to God.

Notice the Little Things

I came across[1] a photo of a a couple of coins and found it an interesting metaphor for marriage. Perhaps nothing is more common place than loose change. I see it everyday and don't give it much thought. Sometimes I drop a nickel or dime and don't even bother to retrieve it.

Yet this picture makes loose change look like something special. The lighting and the sharp focus highlight something that is often overlooked. It reminds me of my little kids who think nickels and dimes are wonderful and treasure each one.

---

[1] http://ahamediqbal.blogspot.com/2006/01/close-to-change.html

After years of marriage, its easy to overlook the little treasures in your relationship. Both the husband and the wife do many little things everyday. Often these little chores, little acts of kindness and little expressions of love go overlooked and under appreciated.

Today stop to consider the importance of the treasure you have and pay your sweetie a compliment (see page 69). Observe something that has previously gone overlooked. Find something your sweetie does then truly and sincerely thank her for it. Put a thank you note on the iron or in the tool box. Hide a small treat or token of affection which will be found while at work. Help out without being asked.

Simple Act of Kindness

A few years ago, I had a bad day. It was early November and we were all getting excited for Thanksgiving and Christmas holidays. Then there was an unexpected company meeting and I found myself unemployed in the middle of an economic slump. Then on my way home from what had been my work, my car died on the side of the freeway.

There I was, standing beside my car on the side of the road, wondering about my car, and concerned about how I was going to take care of my wife and kids when I heard a voice. It startled me because I hadn't even noticed the man stop.

There beside me was a perfect stranger. He asked what was wrong and if he could help. Turns out he keeps a full gas can in his car, "just in case." Soon the car was started and I was on my way. I am forever grateful for that small act of kindness.

What the stranger does not know is how that small act affected me and my family. That simple act changed my whole attitude from "woe is me" to "I can overcome this." One person stopping and noticing a stranded stranger made all the difference in the world.

You can make the difference for your spouse as well. Perform some unexpected act of service for your sweetie. This is particularly effective in high stress situations. Something as simple as doing the dishes when its not your turn or giving them a break can mean so much more than just the value of the act. It can readjust someone's whole view.

Funny thing is, I never even thought to ask the stranger's name.

Altruistic Love Related to Happier Marriages

I came across an article, *Altruistic Love Related to Happier Marriages*[1] that talks about alturism, marriage and happiness. The National Opinion Research Center conducted a study into alturism and published the results.

First what is alturism? The study asked questions like:

"I'd rather suffer myself than let the one I love suffer," and "I'm willing to sacrifice my own wishes to let the one I love achieve his or hers."

This is, are you more interested in your own well-being or that of your sweetheart?

What does this have to do with marriage and romance? The article states:

Among the more altruistic, sixty-seven percent rated their own marriage as "very happy." Among those who were profiled as the least altruistic, only fifty percent said they were very happy in marriage.

We see here a paradox. The less selfish you are, the happier you are. Normally we persue happiness through selfishness. What do I want? What's in it for me? How does this benefit me?

Paradoxially, the road to happines is not "looking out for number one," but making sure your spouse's needs are being met. Happiness comes from serving others, not in being served.

The article also states some othe interesting findings related to empathy (described as feeling protective of others or concerned for the less fortunate):

- Women have a greater feeling of empathy than men
- Children from two-parent homes are more empathetic
- Girls raised by a single father are the least likely to develop empathy
- Financial status bears little on altruism or empathy
- People who vote are more empathetic and altruistic
- Empathy is higher among those who fear crime
- Empathy is higher among those who support increased spending on social programs

Romance comes from looking outward rather than inward.

---

[1] http://news.yahoo.com/s/space/20060209/sc_space/altruisticloverelatedtohappiermarriages

The Folly of Victor Frankenstein

I had never before read Frankenstein. I've seen the various movies based on the book. However, I had never actually sat down and read the book. Well, I corrected that omission. I was reading Frankenstein and was struck by the following:

> I wished, as it were, to procrastinate all that related to my feelings of affection until the great object, which swallowed up every habit of my nature, should be completed.
>
> I then thought that my father would be unjust if he ascribed my neglect to vice, or faultiness on my part; but I am now convinced that he was justified in conceiving that I should not be altogether free from blame. A human being in perfection ought always to preserve a calm and peaceful mind, and never to allow passion or a transitory desire to disturb his tranquility. I do not think that the pursuit of knowledge is an exception to this rule. If the study to which you apply yourself has a tendency to weaken your affections, and to destroy your taste for those simple pleasures in which no alloy can possibly mix, then that study is certainly unlawful, that is to say, not befitting the human mind.

All of us have occupations, studies, hobbies or other interests that demand time, effort and attention. From time to time, these demands may overwhelm other aspects of a balanced life. Long hours of study may be required in educational studies. The pursuit of a career can require many overtime hours. Hobbies have a way of consuming time.

Do not allow these pursuits *to weaken your affections* in your relationship with your partner and your duty to family. The meaning of life can defined in terms of relationships, with the marriage relationship being one of the most important and lasting.

My sweetheart has been very supporting of my career. She understands when I have had to put in lots of overtime and held down the fort when I was traveling and only home every other weekend. However, although she understood the need, it was still difficult to keep the fire burning in our relationship. A relationship requires having the time to discuss the day to day issues as well as working on the romantic aspects. If there is little time for talking, the daily difficulties will dominate the discussion.

Another bit of wisdom: leave work at work. Your sweetheart deserves your full attention. Leave the problems of work at the door. Be focused on what your spouse is saying, not just half listening.

Strive to maintain balance between work, home and other interests.

Just Three Words

Another interesting article I found floating around the Internet:

There are many things that you can do to strengthen your relationships. Often the most effective thing you can do involves saying just three words. When spoken sincerely, these statements often have the power to develop new friendships, deepen old ones and bring healing to relationships that have soured.

The following three-word phrases can be tools to help develop every relationship.

1. Let me help

Good friends see a need and then try to fill it. When they see a hurt they do what they can to heal it. Without being asked, they jump in and help out.

2. I understand you.

People become closer and enjoy each other more when the other person accepts and understands them. Letting your spouse know - in so many little ways - that you understand them, is one of the most powerful tools for healing your relationship. And this can apply to any relationship.

3. I respect you

Respect is another way of showing love. Respect demonstrates that another person is a true equal. If you talk to your children as if they were adults you will strengthen the bonds and become closer friends. This applies to all interpersonal relationships.

4. I miss you.

Perhaps more marriages could be saved and strengthened if couples simply and sincerely said to each other "I miss you." This powerful affirmation tells partners they are wanted, needed, desired and loved. Consider how important you would feel, if you received an unexpected phone call from your spouse in the middle of your workday, just to say "I miss you."

5. Maybe you're right.

This phrase is very effective in diffusing an argument. The implication when you say "maybe you're right" is the humility of admitting, "maybe I'm wrong." Let's face it. When you have an argument with someone, all you normally do is solidify the other person's point of view. They, or you, will not likely change their position and you run the risk of seriously damaging the relationship between you. Saying "maybe you're right" can open the door to explore the subject more. You may then have the opportunity to express your view in a way that is understandable to the other person.

6. Please forgive me

Many broken relationships could be restored and healed if people would admit their mistakes and ask for forgiveness. All of us are vulnerable to faults, foibles and failures. A man should never be ashamed to own up that he has been in the wrong, which is saying, in other words, that he is wiser today than he was yesterday.

7. I thank you.

Gratitude is an exquisite form of courtesy. People who enjoy the companionship of good, close friends are those who don't take daily courtesies for granted. They are quick to thank their friends for their many expressions of kindness. On the other hand, people whose circle of friends is severely constricted often do not have the attitude of gratitude.

8. Count on me

A friend is one who walks in when others walk out. Loyalty is an essential ingredient for true friendship. It is the emotional glue that bonds people. Those that are rich in their relationships tend to be steady and true friends. When troubles come, a good friend is there indicating "you can count on me."

9. I'll be there

If you have ever had to call a friend in the middle of the night, to take a sick child to hospital, or when your car has broken down some miles from home, you will know how good it feels to hear the phrase "I'll be there." Being there for another person is the greatest gift we can give. When we are truly present for other people, important things happen to them and us. We are renewed in love and friendship. We are restored emotionally and spiritually. Being there is at the very core of civility.

10. Go for it

We are all unique individuals. Don't try to get your friends to conform to your ideals. Support them in pursuing their interests, no matter how far out they seem to you. God has given everyone dreams, dreams that are unique to that person only. Support and encourage your friends to follow their dreams. Tell them to "go for it."

11. I love you

Perhaps the most important three words that you can say. Telling someone that you truly love them satisfies a person's deepest emotional needs. The need to belong, to feel appreciated and to be wanted. Your spouse, your children, your friends and you, all need to hear those three little words: "I love you." Love is a choice. You can love even when the feeling is gone.

Mona and Julia

Mona and Julia are old friends. They have both been married for many years. Mona is upset because she thinks her husband doesn't find her attractive anymore. "He doesn't even seem to see me anymore," she cries.

"I'm so sorry for you. My husband says I get more beautiful every day," replies Julia. "Yes," says Mona. "But remember, your husband's an antique dealer."

Vision

I saw this saying: "The best way to predict the future . . . is to create it."

Vision. What do you want your marriage to look like? Take a few minutes and create in your mind the "ideal marriage." Include how you treat each other, expections, and indiviual development. Some areas to include:

- What are my interests and how do I find time to explore them?
- What are my spouse's interests and how do I support her developing them?
- What make me happiest?
- What makes my sweeite happiest?
- How do my children behave?
- How do I express my love and appreciation to my companion?

Picture in your mind the ideal world. Now identify those things **you can change** to bring your marriage closer to your ideal. Start making the changes one at a time.

Do not try and change your spouse. Instead, make the proper changes in your behavior and your sweetie will natuarally make reciprocal changes to adjust.

Love and Joy

Small things, done in great love, bring joy and peace.

— Mother Teresa (1910–1997)

Be Part of Something Beyond Yourself

Being part of an agenda beyond ourselves liberates us to complement each other rather than compete with each other.

— Joseph Stowell

Make your marriage that agenda and find ways to complement (see page 24) your spouse, rather than feeling like you need to compete.

To Appreciate, Communicate & Contemplate

Part of a text of a talk[1] I heard on marriage.

Marriage brings greater possibilities for happiness than does any other human relationship. Yet, some married couples fall short of their full potential. They let their romance become rusty, take each other for granted, allow other interests or clouds of neglect to obscure their vision of what their marriage really could be. Marriages would be happier if nurtured more carefully. Marriage is the foundry for social order, the fountain of virtue and the foundation for eternal exaltation. True marriage is a partnership with God. Three action verbs "to appreciate, to communicate and to contemplate" are helpful in strengthening marriages. Begin with sincere desire. Identify those actions needed to bless your spiritual unity and purpose. Above all, do not be selfish. Generate a spirit of selflessness and generosity. Celebrate and commemorate each day together as a treasured gift from heaven.

— Russell M. Nelson

Compliments are Delightful

Nothing makes people so worthy of compliments as receiving them. One is more delightful for being told one is delightful — just as one is more angry for being told one is angry.

— Katherine F. Gerould

Little kids are a lot of fun. When toddlers are just learing to walk, they fall down a lot. When a child falls, often he looks to the parents to know how to react.

---

[1] http://www.desnews.com/cn/cnf/view/0,2141,445005810,00.html

The the parents are overly concerned, the child will cry. When the parents are not too concerned, the child often laughs and gets back up.A positive reaction will generate positive behavior.

Romantic Bible Verses

Romantic Bible Verses

Take a card and write your sweetheart's name and a Bible reference on it. The fun is in looking up the verses. I have included a few verses for ideas. Looking them up is left as an exercise to the reader.

- Song of Solomon, 2:10–13
- Song of Solomon, 1:15–16
- Song of Solomon, 4:9–15
- Proverbs, 5:18–19
- Proverbs, 31:10–11

Read the Good Book

One aspect of a marriage that is often overlooked is the spiritual side of the relationship. With the pressing demands of the both physical and the emotional needs, the spiritual needs of a couple can be neglected or dismissed altogether. There are always so many things that need doing. Then what little time is left is usually dedicated to meeting emotional needs.

Take time to add a spiritual component to your life and your relationship. A great way to do this is to read from the scriptures together. For those who already have some religion or belief, take some time to study your holy books together as a couple. By fulfilling the spiritual needs, you can add a new dimension to your relationship that you did not know you were missing.

Even if you do not consider any writing to be "The Word of God," your relationship can still benefit. Just pick one of the standard religious texts, be it the Bible, Koran, or some Eastern text. By studying it together you will learn more about yourself and each other.

Ephesians 5

In Ephesians 5:21-33[1] we read:

---

[1] http://scriptures.lds.org/eph/5/21-33#21

21. Submitting yourselves one to another in the fear of God.

22. Wives, submit yourselves unto your own husbands, as unto the Lord.

23. For the husband is the head of the wife, even as Christ is the head of the church: and he is the saviour of the body.

24. Therefore as the church is subject unto Christ, so let the wives be to their own husbands in every thing.

25. Husbands, love your wives, even as Christ also loved the church, and gave himself for it;

26. That he might sanctify and cleanse it with the washing of water by the word,

27. That he might present it to himself a glorious church, not having spot, or wrinkle, or any such thing; but that it should be holy and without blemish.

28. So ought men to love their wives as their own bodies. He that loveth his wife loveth himself.

29. For no man ever yet hated his own flesh; but nourisheth and cherisheth it, even as the Lord the church:

30. For we are members of his body, of his flesh, and of his bones.

31. For this cause shall a man leave his father and mother, and shall be joined unto his wife, and they two shall be one flesh.

32. This is a great mystery: but I speak concerning Christ and the church.

33. Nevertheless let every one of you in particular so love his wife even as himself; and the wife see that she reverence her husband.

There is a lot to think and talk about in these few verses. One thought that goes right to the heart of romance in marriage is: We should think more of our sweetie then ourselves. Husbands are encouraged to treat their wives as Christ treated the church. He sacrificed everything for it. The church was the most important thing. So are our wives are to be most important.

Wives likewise are encourged to submit to and reverence their husbands. Can you think of a more romantic relationship than one where both the husband and wife love each other, respect each other, sacrifice for each other, submit to each other and are truly grateful for each other?

Changing Your Sweetheart

People often complain about their Sweetheart. They say "she just takes me for granted" or "he is not romantic enough." That is usually followed by "if he would only..." or "if she would just change...."

There is so much wrong with that attitude you could write a whole book on it and I'm sure at least one someone has. A better way to change someone's behavior is to change how you act to adjust their reaction. As marriage goes on we fall into patterns and roles. We often act a certain way not because we think its the best way to act, but because it is part of the role we are playing.

Maybe an example will illustrate the point. In the evening when the hubby comes home from work the home may be a bit chaotic. The kids are going every which way with school, homework, sports, etc. The wife is frazzled with all the demands of kids and housewifery. Hubby of course is stressed due to work and frustrated due to traffic. What happens when hubby walks in the door? He might like to have his wife greet him with a smile, pamper him and help him relax. Maybe she could be dressed up waiting for him. The kids are all polished and quietly doing kid things. Likewise, the wife might like some time to talk and have adult communication. She would like some help with the chores and have someone help the kids so she is only doing ten things at once.

Obviously both those things can't happen, so often nothing happens that either spouse really wants. The husband comes home and is unable to unwind. The wife doesn't get the help she needs. So they both collide and spend the evening grumpy with each other. How can it be changed? Try changing yourself.

When the hubby comes home, leave the stress of work and driving in the car. He could take a few moments to relax and be cheerful as he enters the house. Ask his wife how her day was and really **listen**. Share a funny anticdote about the day with her so you can connect. Above all, let the first thing she sees be a smile.

When the wife knows her hubby is about to come home, take a few minutes to destress. Try and find a way to welcome him home and help him destress. Just as with the hubby, be sure to have a smile waiting for him. There is something about a warm and friendly smile that can change everything almost instantly. It seems to say "I am on your side." If your spouse suddenly felt you were on his/her side, wouldn't he/she reciprocate? Try it and see. By breaking out of the mold and doing something for your spouse, you will enable them to break out of their mold and do something for you. Then you will feel like returning the deed, and so on. This can create an upward spiral of goodwill and gratitude to replace the downward spiral of resentment and ingratitude.

Remember: "It is by small and simple things are great things brought to pass; and small means in many instances doth confound the wise." Don't try and do some huge change, just a small change applied consistently.

Reverse Golden Rule

We have all heard the "golden rule." It is found in Matthew 7:12[1]:

1. Therefore all things whatsoever ye would that men should do to you, do ye even so to them: for this is the law and the prophets.

We have to think about it as treating people the way we want to be treated. There is also an implied corollary to the golden rule. It is that people reflect back the treatment they receive. A couple of examples to illustrate the point. First, smile. When you smile at someone they will smile back. Try it. It works on perfect strangers walking down the street. Second, expectations. If you expect someone to fail they often will. If you expect someone to succeed, they often will. Why? Think about it. How do you treat someone whom you expect to fail? How do you treat someone whom you expect to succeed?

The Heart Nebula

The night sky is full of wonders and one of them is The Heart Nebula[2] also known as IC 1805—The Heart Nebula in Cassiopeia. A grand cosmic valentine

---

[1] http://scriptures.lds.org/matt/7/12#12
[2] http://www.allaboutastro.com/ic1805.html

for the whole world to enjoy given by the great Creator who loves us. I John 4:7[1] reminds us:

> 7. Beloved, let us love one another: for love is of God; and every one that loveth is born of God, and knoweth God.

Go With Him Twain

In Matthew 5:41[2] it says:

> 41. And whosoever shall compel thee to go a mile, go with him twain.

This is often referred to as "going the extra mile." Do more than is necessary or asked of you.

How does this apply to romance in marriage? There are several aspects that could be explored, but a simple example will suffice for today. I was serving as "Toastmaster" for the week in the Toastmasters[3] club at work. The Toastmaster is in charge of the meeting, including the theme. The meeting happened to fall close to St. Patricks day. I decided to decorate the room with a pile of gold coin candy.

My wife was headed to the store and asked if I needed anything. I mentioned that if she came across some of those candies to pick them up for me. Well, she was at the store for quite a bit longer than I had expected. Turns out she had to go to half a dozen stores to find the candies. She also got other St. Patricks day decorations for me to use.

Thanks sweetie! You are great at going with me twain.S

Today and Forever

I Corinthians 11:11

> 11. Nevertheless neither is the man without the woman, neither the woman without the man, in the Lord.

---

[1] http://scriptures.lds.org/1_jn/4/7#7
[2] http://scriptures.lds.org/matt/5/41#41
[3] http://www.toastmasters.org/

On television and in movies we often hear the person officiating a marriage ceremony repeat the phrase "until death do you part." Does the relationship between man and wife really only last until one or the other dies? Are we not together as husband and wife in the here-after?

During the Easter season when we remember the resurrection of the Savior and the hope it gives for a better here-after. For me, that hope includes being with my beloved companion for all eternity. As it says in Corinthians, "neither is the man without the woman." When the time comes that one of us passes on, that parting is not permanent. Instead, it is just a short time until we can be together forever.

Be Benevolent to Each Other

In Bill and Ted's Excellent Adventure Bill (or is it Ted?), advises the people of the future to:

Be Excellent! ... to each other.

That thought, by itself should be sufficient for an article. But wait, there is more. In 1 Corinthians 7:3[1], Paul advises the saints in Corinth:

3. Let the husband render unto the wife due benevolence: and likewise also the wife unto the husband.

What, then, is benevolence? One definition is: *The disposition to do good; good will; charitableness; love of mankind, accompanied with a desire to promote their happiness.* In other words, a desire to do nice things to make other people happy. It is the ability to find joy in making other people happy. It is the very opposite of "what's in it for me?"

Benevolence, then, is what romance is all about. By doing acts of benevolence for your sweetie and by recognizing and appreciating benevolence when directed at you, you will discover the very heart and soul of romance. Indeed, the very key to keeping the fire going and the honeymoon alive. Amazing how things haven't really changed in 2,000 years.

Be Benevolent! ... to each other.

---

[1] http://scriptures.lds.org/1_cor/7/3

Treasure

In Matthew 6:21[1] we read:

> For where your treasure is, there will your heart be also.

My sweetie is one of my greatest treasures because that is where my heart is. How do you tell where a person's heart is? A man shows what is important by how he spends his money, his time and his energies. We all have a lot of financial and temporal demands, but somehow we make time for the things that are important. Make sure that some of that time is spent on your most important treasure, your spouse.

Improve Communication Within Your Marriage

I have a difficult time recommending web-sites that deal with the topic of romance while still being family friendly. As you can imagine, most romance sites are not family friendly. Today, I have found a site I think can add to your marriage and your family. It is the Family Site at mormon.org[2].

As you may or may not know, The Church of Jesus Christ of Latter-day Saints[3] (or Mormons) is a big supporter of families[4]. For this reason, they have provided this website as a public service. It is just what it appears to be. There will not be any missionaries knocking on your door as a result of looking at this website. Feel free to take a look.

Here are some things to consider:

- Keep problems private—when you need to discuss a serious concern with your spouse, do it "behind closed doors"
- Listen—be patient and respectful while your spouse is speaking
- Learn to negotiate—different perspectives can strengthen your relationship—be willing to compromise

---

[1] http://scriptures.lds.org/matt/6/21#21
[2] http://family.mormon.org/
[3] http://lds.org/
[4] http://www.mormon.org/learn/0,8672,1149-1,00.html

- Keep talking; openly discuss challenges and desires
- *A soft answer turneth away wrath* (Proverbs 15:1); When voices are raised, problems become more complicated—a gentle response can bring peace, understanding and love.

A Soft Answer Turneth Away Wrath

It is in the home that our behavior is most significant. It is the place where our actions have the greatest impact, for good or ill. Sometimes we are so much "at home" that we no longer guard our words. It is easy forget simple civility, common courtesy and mutual respect. If we are not on guard, we can fall into the habit of criticizing one another, losing our tempers, or behaving selfishly. Because they love us, our spouses and children may be quick to forgive, but they often carry away in silence unseen injuries and unspoken heartache.

Your sweetie should know how much you love them by how you speak. Do love and courtesy garnish your words? Do your body language and "tone of voice" communicate your appreciation for your sweetheart?

Here are two simple ways to improve communication. First, smile. I hve written about smiling several times. Smile at your sweetie. Second, look each other in the eye. It increases the feeling of sincerity.

Proverbs 15

In Proverbs 15:1 we read (emphasis added):

A *soft* answer turneth away wrath: but grievous words stir up anger.

What happens when someone raises their voice to you? Naturally you yell back at them. It is human nature to match the tone of the answer to the tone of the question. Often this leads to an argument where one is neither needed nor intended. If you yell at me, I'll yell at you—the same mentality as "an eye for an eye," which leaves the whole world blind.

Instead of yelling, answer in a softer voice. A softer voice does not sound angry. You must listen harder to hear a soft voice. As Wayne S. Peterson once said:

Our home should ideally be a refuge where each member feels safe, secure, loved, and insulated from harsh criticism and contention that we so often encounter in the world.

Ecclesiastes 9

Live joyfully with the wife whom thou lovest all the days of the life...

Ecclesiastes 9:9

Move beyond living together and live joyfully together. Make your spouse laugh. Share your goals and dreams while helping your sweetheart to fulfill your those of your mate. **Smile**. Express gratitude in word and in deed.

Matthew 5

I normally avoid the "thou shalt not" in favor of the "thou shalt" in all my articles. Telling someone what the wrong answer is, is not the same as giving them the right answer. Also, having a positive approach can be more encouraging and gives my writing as a whole a more uplifting attitude.

Today, I am going to break with my custom and go with a "thou shalt not." In Matthew 5:28[1] we read:

> 28. But I say unto you, that whosoever looketh on a woman to lust after her hath committed adultery with her already in his heart.

For several months this verse had been popping into my brain so I finally decided to write about it.

There is a lot of salacious material available on the Internet, in magazines and in movies. I could harp on how indulging in such material destroys your self-confidence, is addicting and reduces the respect your sweetheart and children have for you. There has been a lot written on the subject, so I don't need to address it here.

Instead, I will address the issue of trust and fidelity. Trust is essential to a happy and romantic marriage. Anything that compromises trust necessarily erodes the very foundation of a marriage. Contrariwise, anything that builds

---

[1] http://scriptures.lds.org/matt/5/28#28

trust, strengths the marriage. Spend your time being faithful and 100% committed to your sweetie. Strengthen the foundation of your relationship a little at a time rather than weakening it.

A last note: My wife and I read a quote from a marriage counselor stating that 90% of couples in counseling are there due to lapses in fidelity.

Gifts and Surprises

Ambush Getaway

Before my wife and I were married, her father offered to give us the money for the reception if we would elope. I am not sure how serious he was, he likes to joke with us. We sometimes wonder what it would have been like to elope, just sneak off and get married. There is something romantic about the idea of just getting away on the spur of the moment.

Its not too late to do that, even if you have been married for a long time. Plan an "Ambush Getaway". Make all the arrangements including reservations at a hotel, finding someone to watch the kids overnight, pack for your sweetie. Then, "kidnap" your sweetheart and enjoy some time together.

"S.H.M.I.L.Y."

Have you ever heard of the acronym S.H.M.I.L.Y. . . . . See How Much I Love You. By using only this acronym you can take turns leaving little reminders of your love for each other. It is more fun if you get creative: Write it on the bathroom mirror with soap, hide a small note in a sock, shoe or sandwich, use Oreos on the back window of your sweethearts car. The trick is to not be too obvious. Think of places to hide the notes where your sweetheart will find them at a later time. For example, pack them in a lunchbox to be found at work.

Until the Last Flower Fades

Give your sweetheart a dozen real roses and one silk rose with a note that says: "I will love you until the last flower fades."

Small, Sweet Surprises

Buy several small candies, the one's your sweetie really likes, and hide them in various places so your sweetheart will find them over the course of a week.

Make a Note of It

Throughout the year that special someone in your life will make comments like "Oh, I've always wanted one of those," "I just know we could never get that" or "maybe someday . . .". You get the idea. This is known as hint dropping. When a hint it dropped, make a note of it.

First, get yourself a notepad, or just a page in a day planner or some spot in your PDA. Call it your "hint list." Next, whenever a hint is dropped, log it in the hint list. Then, next time you feel like doing something special, take one of the things off the hint list and make it happen.

Covered in Warmth

Before your sweetie gets into the shower, start the dryer going with some towels. Just as they are finishing, get two towels out of the dryer and leave them for her. A nice warm towel after showering is a luxury she may not have experienced before.

Piecing it Together

Take a favorite photo of the two of you together and make a copy of it. On the back write a note explaining why this pictures means so much to you. Be sure to include that your spouse is still very important to you. Then cut it up as a jigsaw puzzle, put it in an envelope, and mail it to you sweetie.

Remember Me at Work

If your sweetie has to work outside the home, hide a nice note in their lunch or briefcase. Be sure they will find the note while they are away from you. Also be sure to given them a warm welcome home after work.

What is a "nice" note? Make romantic and intimate as you want. The more personal the better.

Create your own Holiday

Days off work are precious things. We get so few a year that we often hoard them. To completely surprise your sweetie, take a day off work just to spend together. You need not have any special plans, just spending a day together can convert the most mundane chores into quality "us" time.

Of course, if you can do something to get away for a few hours, that would be great to.

Sometimes the kids get a day off from school. For a special family time, take one of those days off and enjoy the day with the kids as well.

Asking

Find a time when you need to ask your sweetie a question. Instead of just asking it, write it on a piece of paper. Preface your question with a compliment like:

Sweetie,
You have lovely eyes, I am so lucky to have you. Where is the sugar?
XOXOXOX

A Frosty Message

During winter months, scraping frost off the car windows becomes part of the morning ritual. If your spouse has to scrape the frost off the windows before leaving, you have a couple of opportunities to surprise him. One thing to do is to write a message to him in the frost on the windows. The message could be a heart with both your initials in it. Keep it simple and short so the letters can be large and easily seen.

On another day, sneak out and scrape the windows for your sweetie. Leave a note on the steering wheel. Something like: "Your smile warms a frosty morning."

The Gift of Time

Without any fanfare and without having to be asked, do some chore or task that your sweetie normal does or has been avoiding doing. It need not be something big—just a small thing like doing the dishes, helping with homework, or changing a light bulb. By doing this you will be giving your sweetheart the greatest gift of all: extra time to do other things.

Note on the Windshield

Leave a note on your sweetie's windshield. If possible, do it away from home so that it is even less expected. Try leaving the note on the car at your sweetheart's work or while they are at the store or running some other errand.

VIP

Imagine you were going to meet someone very important. It could be someone famous, your boss or someone else you would like to impress. How would you prepare for such a meeting? You would go all out to look your best and make a good impression.

Isn't your spouse a very important person? Every now again, prepare yourself for your spouse like you would for that person you wanted to impress. Let your spouse know how important he is to you.

Gift Cards

My wife loves to shop, but doesn't often go shopping for herself. With what kids need, car and home repairs, medical bills and so forth, there isn't a lot of money to go shopping with and she often feels guilty if she spends anything on herself. Even if I give her cash for birthday or Mother's Day, she will often spend it on something the kids need or want.

One thing that works are gift cards from a store where she likes to shop. Sometimes gift cards feel impersonal. They seem to say "I don't really know you well enough to choose a gift you would like." For that reason I try to avoid giving gift cards to people. But in the case of my sweetheart, it works out well. First, I spent the money so she doesn't have to feel guilty about it. Second, since it can only be used at a place she likes[1] to go, she can't spend it on the kids. Third, she likes me to accompany her when she shops so it makes a nice date night (see page 73) for her. Lastly, it lets her know I am paying attention (see page 1) to what she likes.

Of course, getting a gift card is lots easier than trying to decide which size and what color to buy. Works out nice for both the person giving the card and the person receiving the card.

Friday the Baker's Dozen-eth

Here it is again, Friday the 13th, namesake of a lot of really bad movies. Maybe that is why the day is considered unlucky because it makes you think of awful cinema. I'm sure there are other reasons for the Friday the 13th superstition that you could find if you just looked[2] in different places[3].

Unless your sweetie suffers from *triskaidekaphobia*[4], the day makes a good time for a surprise gift for your sweetheart. A while ago it was suggested (see page 59):

> Give your sweetheart a dozen real roses and one silk rose with a note that says "I will love you until the last flower fades."

For whatever reason, we like to think in terms of "a dozen." Many things come in dozens likes eggs, donuts, and flowers. Today's tip is to turn the common place dozen into a special dozen plus one, a baker's dozen if you will. The trick is to make the "plus one" stand out as a surprise as in the above idea. The note focuses the attention on the one flower that will last forever, just like your love. How romantic.

Some other ideas for a dozen plus one:

- A balloon bouquet with twelve regular balloons and a single Mylar balloon
- A dozen roses with a single daisy

---

[1] http://www.coldwatercreek.com/
[2] http://www.rosslyntemplars.org.uk/friday,_13th.htm
[3] http://www.infoplease.com/spot/friday13th.html
[4] http://dictionary.reference.com/wordoftheday/archive/2005/05/13.html

- Twelve Hershey's kisses with a note where to get the other kiss
- Twelve romantic coupons with an extra one hand made by you (the extra one could be something more personalized for your sweetie, or it could be a fill in the blank one so your sweetheart could say what the coupon is to be used for)
- A dozen suckers (think Dum Dum or Tootsie Pops) and a giant heart shaped sucker
- This one is a bit obscure: Get a picture of the two of you, make a copy and write a note on the back, cut it into twelve pieces and hide them where your sweetie will find them; once assembled they will create the thirteenth—your note
- Make a CD with twelve of your sweethearts favorite tracks—make the 13th track either you singing, playing an instrument or just even you talking and telling your sweetie how much he/she is loved and appreciated

Sending Secret Messages

Miguel de Cervantes (a sixteenth century spanish novelist) once wrote:

> That which costs little is less valued.

That is that people tend to undervalue things that cost them little. The cost of a thing may be in money, yet this is not the only way that cost is calculated. Time and effort are also used to deteremine cost and are often considered more pecious than money. The correllary is that a higher cost brings a higher value. Something that cost a lot of money, or took a lot of time and effort, is held with higher regard.

Saying "thank you" or even writing "I love you" can be easily dismissed. Its not the sentiment is not sincere, but that the message costs little in the sending and in the receiving. If the cost of sending the message and the cost of receiving the message are increased, the message itself will be more valued.

The cost here is not in money, but in time and effort. By using a secret code, you can send a message that will have a higher value because of the increased effort in writing it and reading it. Here are a few ideas:

- Verses from the bible (see page 47) (just send the reference and have your sweetie look them up)
- ROT-13[1] is a simple code in which letters of the alphabet are replaced by other letters (see rot13.com[2] for a web page to do the converting for you)
- Use a different alphabet to write like cirith[3]
- A message treasure hunt: Create the message as a set of instructions for finding the words that form the message (the clues would be: book page paragraph word—for instance: Moby Dick, page one, paragraph one, word one = "Call")
- Do the last one using bible book, chapter, verse and word

Gubh funyg syveg srebpvbhfyl rnpu qnl jvgu gul fcbhfr gung gul zneevntr funyy or oyrffrq jvgu fgeratgu, wbl naq ybatrivgl.

Celebrating Your Sweetie as a Parent

The most important task most of us will ever perform is that of mother or father. As a society, we understand better than ever the social implications if either father or mother is missing from the home. Yet, that same society diminishes the importance of parenthood, making it seem secondary to other pursuits such as career or "personal fulfillment."

On top of that, being a parent is often a thankless duty. Children are notoriously ungrateful. At least until they leave home and really realize what their parents both did and sacrificed on their behalf. Yet most of us wouldn't trade parenthood for anything. We love our children and the joy they bring into our lives. The sacrifices are made without even thinking, just because our kids need something.

For example, when the kids are in school almost all my free time is dedicated to helping my kids with homework. I am now spending lots more time on homework than I ever spent while going to school. Silly me, I thought when I graduated I would be done doing homework. Mother's Day and Father's Day are both long gone. On Mother's Day you have to say nice things about your

---

[1] http://en.wikipedia.org/wiki/ROT13
[2] http://www.rot13.com/index.php
[3] http://www.omniglot.com/writing/cirth.htm

wife, because its expected. Same with Father's Day. The message of how much you appreciate and love your sweetheart is dulled by the duty of the day. Everyone is forced to say those things so the sincerity is lost. Also, there is no spontaneity.

Now would be a good time to celebrate what a wonderful father or mother your sweetie is. It will be completely unexpected and seem more sincere because no one is making you do it. One of the best things you could do would be to write a letter of love and appreciation for what a great parent your sweetie is and present it to your sweetheart with some flowers or chocolates, both of which are cheaper this time of year. Let your sweetie know that at least one person recognizes and appreciates all the work, worry and sacrifice that goes into being a parent.

Preparing to be Spontaneous

Has this ever happened to you? You feel particularly grateful to your sweetie and want to do something extra special to show how much you feel. You think up something, but of course you don't have that around the house. Then you run to the store only to find that they don't have what you are looking for. You end up spending a lot of time and not being able to do what you wanted to do anyway. So now, instead of feeling grateful, you're feeling frustrated. What you need is a "spontaneity kit." This kit is a collection of simple things that will allow you to do something special for your sweetie on a moment's notice. My kit includes:

- "I Love You" stickers (these are little round stickers in lots of colors)
- Candles—both scented and otherwise
- CDs with romantic music
- DVDs we both appreciate
- Heart shaped box (i.e., the box that Valentines chocolates come in)
- Index cards with various romantic thoughts on them—hand written by me
- Massage Oil
- Blank greeting cards with romantic, friendship and appreciation themes
- Chocolate Kisses and Hugs (ok, I don't really have any of these on hand, but I should!)

Of course, my kit isn't completely all hidden. The DVDs and CDs are just part of our collection. The candles are some she bought that she likes. The other things I keep hidden to surprise my sweetie every now and again.

I use things out of my kit fairly regularly. For example, my sweetie had misplaced a small item and couldn't find it. While she was gone, I happened across it. Rather than just give it to her when she returned, I placed it in the heart-shaped box with a small love letter and left it on her pillow. She wondered what was in the box and was pleasantly surprised when it was the misplaced item with a note. Another simple example: My sweetie has medication she takes daily. I stuck two of the *I Love You* stickers on the lid so she would remember each day that she is loved.

This last example of using the kit even surprised me. The other day I got home and my "I Love You" stickers were out. My kids are curious and I often include them in my little romantic gestures. Therefore, I wasn't too surprised that one of the kids had been looking at them. After all, they are fun and there are quite a number of them in the package, so I could spare a few. Well, it turns out that my wife was having a bad day and my youngest had gotten a sticker and given it to her to help her have a better day. Sometimes a sticker says it better, I guess.

Some of these things are only available at Valentine's Day. So the idea is to keep your eyes open for things to add to your spontaneity kit throughout the year. A collection of items allows you to take better advantage of the opportunities that come your way.

Enrichment

I took a couple of the kids to the zoo the other day. As I think I mentioned before, we have a family pass to the local zoo. We end up at the zoo quite often and spend a couple of hours there.

The last time we went, they were having an "enrichment" day for the animals. What that meant is that there was something different for the animals. The idea was to stimulate the animals both physically and mentally. The little Golden Lion Tamarins had food hidden in paper bags. Other monkeys had new things to climb on or play with. The penguins had their fish thrown into the water and they had to go swim and get it. They didn't seem to catch on very well, at least at first.

As part of this animal enrichment, there were various activities for the kids and signs with explanations of the various enrichment activities. One of these signs caught my attention. It was a sign answering why they don't give the animals the toys, puzzles and other things everyday. If the items were given to the animals everyday, they would stop serving their purpose, providing stimulation to the animals. In essence, the animals would get used to having them. It is novelty of the item that makes the difference.

While we are not animals, we also get used to the things in our lives. Even something we really enjoy can become boring through constant repetition. For example, if your sweetie likes flowers, receiving them occasionally will be a special treat. But if they were received everyday, they would soon become boring.

The moral of the story is to not do the same thing all the time. Do the unexpected. Give flowers on a non-holiday instead of a holiday. Send a card "just because." Do the dishes or some chore you don't normally do. Challenge the daily routine, once in a while.

What's Better than a Nice Warm Bath?

A nice warm towel (see page 60) afterwards.

I love autumn with the warm days, cool evenings and crisp mornings. However, getting out of the shower is a bit of a shock, *Brrrr*! Do something thoughtful for your sweetie, provide them with a nice warm towel. If you have never tried it, do so. It is luxurious.

Take a Moment

One night I was treated to a beautiful moon-rise. As it came up over the mountains, it was almost full and very bright. The wispy clouds combined with the light to give the evening an ethereal feel to it. And I almost missed it.

My wife came home and called me out into the yard. The kids were looking out the window to see what mom and dad were up to and I was a bit puzzled myself. My weife walked me out into the street and showed me the lovely moon and beautiful evening. We stood for a moment, admiring the scene and enjoying each others company. The air was just cool enough to make holding each other very pleasant. It was well worth a couple of minutes of time.

Tonight, take a minute, just for the two of you. Hold hands, hug and enjoy.

Break the Routine

Sometimes we get trapped by routine. We do the same thing everyday, day-in and day-out. We are like little robots that get up, go to work, come home, eat, do chores, kids do homework, etc. By the end of the day, we are so tired, we go to bed and start it all over tomorrow.

As I've mentioned before, this sort of thing can take the fire out of a marriage. Fortunately, by breaking out of the routine, just a little bit, you can start to fix that.

What can you do to break out of a routine? Try thinking of the things you "used to do." You know, before the kids came. Maybe brushing your sweetie's hair or giving a foot rub. When was the last time you wrote your sweetheart a little love letter?

Well, back to kids and homework.

Pay your Sweetie a Compliment

Pay your sweetie a compliment (see page 18), just make sure it is a sincere one. Think of some physical feature you are attracted to, some talent they possess, or some other aspect of your sweetie that is really wonderful.

Now, write the compliment down and send it to your sweetheart via snail-mail. People often feel the need to argue with a compliment to keep from appearing arrogant. You can't argue with the written word. Also, it makes the compliment seem more sincere as it has a physical incarnation. Talk is cheap.

Or you could just post it in your blog or include it in a book you are writing: *Sweetie, you have the most beautiful eyes. Our kids are so lucky to have inherited them from you.*

For a funny compliment, see Surrealist Compliments For All[1].

---

[1] http://m0smith.freeshell.org/blog-humor/2005/11/surrealism-server-surrealist.html

An Open Love Letter

Previously, I wrote about love letters. I just came across a wonderful example[1] of a love letter. Here is a small excerpt:

> You once asked me if I would do it all again. In spite of everything, dear, the answer is yes; because all of it happened with **you**.

[1] http://cancertalk.blogspot.com/2006/02/open-letter-to-my-husband.html

Date Ideas

Date Night

Remember when you were dating how much fun it was? Dating is an important part of courtship. It can be just as important for married couples. Are you the same person you before you were married? Is your sweetie the same person you married? Since the only constant in the universe is change, it stands to reason that each of you have changed. What better way to keep from feeling "who is this person" than dating. It only make sense. Dating is how you each learned about each other in the first place.

Dates have the following benefits:

- Shared experiences. Some "we" time is important
- A chance to talk
- Have fun together
- Laugh
- Continue to get to know each other

S'More

Most everyone loves s'mores. After all, what's not to love about the ooey, gooey, crunchy, chocolatey delicacy? Most often s'mores are done over a camp fire in the great outdoors. Tthe smell of the smoke and forest with the sounds of the fire crackling add to the overall enjoyment of these treats. However, even if you are not camping, there are several ways to enjoy s'mores.

Microwave

Place a graham cracker on a flat micro-wave safe plate. Then place the chocolate on top of it. Finally, place the marshmallow on the chocolate. Place the plate in the microwave and nuke for a few seconds until the marshmallow starts to expand. **WATCH IT CAREFULLY!** It only takes thirteen seconds in my microwave at home. The marshmallow will expand like a balloon. Take it out, put the other half of the graham cracker on top and share. For added ambience, get one of those scented candles that smells outdoorsy and light it—maybe even one of those fireplace screen savers on your computer.

Charcoal

S'mores prepared on charcoal briquettes can be a lot of fun. First, it takes some time to get them going so it can be a great way to just sit, relax and enjoy some time together. Then, with the controlled heat of the briquettes, its easier to make the "perfect" marshmallow. Instead of cooking your own marshmallow, cook one for each other and try to make them "perfect." Then make a great show of enjoying it.

Watching a Movie

Of course, spending time watching a movie together can be romantic. But it needs to be a good "couple watchable" movie. If the movie is a pure "chick flick" then he might be bored. On the other hand, violence, gore and flying body parts don't set the proper mood either. The best romantic movies portray the nobility of the human spirit. A few of the most romantic movies to watch together are:

- The Princess Bride
- Casablanca
- A Walk in the Clouds
- The Mask of Zorro
- First Knight

Caramel Apples

Apples are in season the the fall but you can get them all year round. What better way to spend some time together than with caramel apples? They are a delightful treat, not too sweet and mostly good for you. There are several ways to enjoy them.

- Go to one of the "gourmet" candy places in town together. They usually have gourmet caramel apples in a variety a of flavors that they will cut into slices for you. Be bold, be daring, pick a flavor have never tried and share it together. These candy stores are often in a shopping mall so the apple can be a part of an evening of holding hands, window shopping, laughing and trying something new.

- Pick up a gourmet caramel apple on the way home and surprise your sweetie. Take turns feeding slicesof the apple to each other.
- At most grocery stores they have caramel apple kits in the fruit department by the apples. These include sheets of caramel and sticks. The procedure is simple. Wrap the apple with the caramel, harpoon it using the stick and nuke it for a few seconds. Try buying one each of several varieties of apples and have a taste test of which variety makes the best treat.

Season to Fall In Love

What a great time of year autumn is! The weather cools off and in many parts of the country the trees are doing a slow motion fireworks display. Here in our neck of the woods there are several "scenic loops" that are famous for their fall colors. Recently I took off early from work and took my sweetheart for a drive on one of these scenic loops. The fall colors were amazing against the deep green of the evergreens. We even spotted a couple of moose near the highest point of the road. It will be one of those times we will remember and talk about for many years.

Be sure and bring a camera and get some pictures of each other in the fall beauty. Take some time to get out of the car and walk among the trees and the leaves. The smell of the cool air, the colors of the trees, the crunch of the leaves underfoot, and the feel of holding hands can make autumn a feast for the senses.

Sunrise, Sunset

In early fall, the sun gets up later and goes to bed earlier each day. The last couple of weeks before the shift to daylight savings are a great time to do something few couples take time to do: watch the sun rise. The sun comes up pretty late so you don't even have to get up early. Have yourselves a warm breakfast. Then make some nice hot cocoa and go outside and spend a few minutes counting the stars, watching them disappear, and seeing the sun peep over the horizon.

Can't manage a sunrise? Try a sunset instead. Sunsets are also worth a few minutes with your sweetie. If you have the kids along, have them try and name all the colors they see.

Batter Up!

Have you ever been to one of those batting cages? The ones around here have different cages with pitching machines that throw either softballs or regular baseballs. The pitching is either fast, medium or slow. The slow pitch was slow enough that even a first grader was able to hit it a couple of times. Each of you can take turns hitting a few pitches while the other provides the cheering section. A great way for the just the two of you or the whole family to have a good time and not spend too much money.

Sharing a Secret

Admit it, there are some "secrets" that you share with your sweetie. Not the "dirty laundry" kind of secrets, but the fun secrets that no one knows about. Things like that one song that is "your song" or that little restaurant that no one knows about but has a great Italian food and the accordion player on Friday nights. The secret discoveries that couples share over the years are what these shared secrets are all about.

One fun shared secret can be a movie. It needs to be a movie that is not the most popular movie du jour. Instead, your secret can be a lesser known film that no one knows about, or its not a secret. It can be a fun independent movie that you see at some film festival. Also, DVDs can make for some "shared secret" movies. Just be adventuresome and try a movie you have not seen before. Romantic comedies are often the best for a couple who want to enjoy watching a movie and being together.

If you want a suggestion, let me recommend "Our Hospitality" starring Buster Keaton. It is an old silent romantic comedy with two feuding families. Of course, the son of one family falls for the daughter of the other, not realizing they are mortal enemies. I'm not going to say anymore except that it is one of the funniest movies I have ever seen. The humor includes the broad physical comedy Buster Keaton is famous for, the standard young couple overcoming adversity and a very clever play of feuding and hospitality. But the train scene brought tears to my eyes.

When discovering a new "shared secret" movie be sure to set the mood. Take the time to make some movie popcorn and have everything proper for some good movie watching while snuggling. Having a shared secret is as much about how you felt while discovering the shared secret as what you were discovering.

High School Play

A lot of schools and community theaters stage plays at various times throughout the year. School plays and community theater make great, inexpensive dates. You are not going to see great Broadway acting and props, but you will see something interesting. It is a great way to support the school or local arts organization and get out at the same time. We have taken our older kids and made it a fun family outing as well.

Date Night at Home

Do you have a lock on your bedroom door? Of course you have a lock on the bedroom door. For a date one night put a sign on the bedroom door that reads
> "Mom and Dad are on a date tonight and will be home around 9:00 p.m.. Pretend they are not home."

Then go in the bedroom, lock the door and watch a movie together. Don't have a TV in the room? Even better! Have a pillow fight, or make big plans for fantasy vacations. Just talk and laugh together. Kids not old enough to watch themselves? That's ok, just get a babysitter like you would if you were really going out for your date.

Watching the Sunset

Spring is a wonderful time of year. I should write an Ode to Spring[1] but there are lots of them and those better than my attempts at poetry. I digress.

---

[1] http://www.google.com/search?q=Ode+to+Spring

Spring is a great time for you and your sweetie to watch the sunset together. The sun goes down late enough to get home from work and still have enough time to prepare. It goes down early enough to not make too late of an evening. There is still a hint of chill in the air to make snuggling very pleasant.

Instructions for watching the sunset:

- Find out when sunset[1] is going to be
- Find a suitable location (some ideas might be up on a hill with a good view to the west, a restaurant that has a good view to the west or over some body of water—its not that important)
- Bring a some treats like chocolate or cookies and milk (something small and portable—maybe even a picnic dinner)
- Bring a blanket to sit and snuggle together
- Plan to arrive and have everything ready fifteen minutes before the grand event
- Sit, eat, talk, snuggle and enjoy the show!

Candlelight Dinner for Two

To add romance to a meal, try adding candlelight. People associate candlelight with special occasions. By adding candlelight to an ordinary meal, it becomes special. Of course, using the fine china, a table cloth and preparing a special meal (or getting take out) adds to the sense of romance. Don't forget to dress up, even though the meal is at home.

Why do we like fire? Whether it is the flicker of a candle, the warm glow of a camp fire or the blaze of a bonfire, most people love fire. The flicking flames add a dramatic flare to a meal. The dancing shadows add a sense of energy to the meal, a romantic dynamic if you will. The glimmer of the candle catches the eye while it casts a flattering glow upon your sweetheart. All these visual clues equate to an enhanced sense of wonder and mystery.

Everyone seems to look better in candlelight. Every notice how a flame seems to make your sweetheart's eyes twinkle as they smile? The natural light

---

[1] http://www.worldtime.com/

of a fire seems to draw out a natural beauty in the skin that is otherwise hidden under artificial lighting. A burning candle seems to put people in a better mood, which makes them smile more.

A candlelight dinner is wonderful as a couple only activity. If you can't have the house yourselves, maybe you can arrange it somewhere else, or even outdoors. Also, a special candlelight dinner can be fun for the whole family.

Watching the Sunset, Part II

A previous article (see page 77) discussed an idea for a romantic date centered around watching the sunset. Today, I continue the idea using a different approach.

Most cities have restaurants that have great views of the sunset. A fine meal in a romantic setting can lead to sharing a memorable evening together. Maybe even surprise your sweetie with a small gift or card expressing love and gratitude. Give your gift as the sun sets.

Finding a good sunset-viewing restaurant is not all that hard. Hotels and other tall building in town are good places to start. Ask friends and family for good restaurants with a view. Sometimes out-of-the way restaurants have a nice west facing window.

Finally, sometimes these restaurants are "go there for the view" restaurants. The food does not have to be good if the restaurant has a great enough view. If that is the case, consider going there for dessert. That way the whole evening is not spoiled by a poor quality meal.

GPS Scavenger Hunt

With new technology, we can up date the old scavenger hunt by using a GPS (Global Positioning System) receiver. A GPS can tell you within ten feet where you are anywhere on earth. They have a lot of uses and can be real fun.

For the scavenger hunt, get the GPS position for several memorable places from your courtship and marriage. Examples include where your first date was, where you first kissed, where you were married, and your favorite restaurant. Once you have the location of each place, there are several ways to do the scavenger hunt.

Leave your sweetie the GPS and a note to go to the first location. At that location, have another note directing them to the second location and so on. Be waiting at the last location which could be a restaurant, theater or even back home.

Do the same as above, but rather than having each location be some spot from your past, make each location part of the evening. Give him/her a list of locations and what to do there. The list would be:

- Location 1: get flowers
- Location 2: get dessert
- Location 3: get dinner (have it pre-ordered)
- Location 4: get romantic (be waiting here)

Give your date the list of places to go and the GPS and let them navigate while you drive. Have them give you directions; pretend you don't know where you are supposed to turn. The list of locations could be memorable places from your marriage or part of a progressive date: restaurant, theater, dessert, home.

Of course, make sure sweetie knows how to use GPS before sending them alone on a scavenger hunt. Also, have some way for sweetie to contact you in case of getting lost.

A Long Lunch

As the children get older, it can be hard to find time to be alone with your spouse. Children have school, sports, friends, homework, and so much more. The parents end up spending a lot of time driving kids to events, watching sports and performances and encouraging them in homework. When is there time for each other?

One way to be alone together is to have a lunch date. Make arrangements to have lunch together. If you work close enough to home, a lunch at home can be fun and inexpensive. If not, you can either pick up your sweetie at work and go someplace close to work or you can arrange to meet each other at a restaurant.

It can be a lot easier to get together for lunch than for dinner, especially if the kids are in school.

Audrey Hepburn

Its usually not a good idea to talk about other women when you are trying to be romantic, however in this case I will make an exception. Audrey Hepburn[1] was in a lot of classic movies like: "Charade", "My Fair Lady", "Sabrina" and "Wait Until Dark". If you are looking for a great romantic movie to watch together with your sweetie, these films make great choices.

Geocaching

If you have a GPS a fun date or family activity can be geocaching[2]. Never heard of geocaching? Think of it as a giant treasure hunt. People have "hidden" various objects all over and registered their coordinates on web-sites like http://www.geocaching.com/[3]. You go to the website, put in your zip-code and get a list of objects hidden in and around your city. Each has the coordinates to find it using a GPS as well as a description like:

> Placed in a park stip in West Bountiful. Weary travelers rejoice! This small tupperware is in camo to hide it well. Shouldn't be too hard to find otherwise. While you are around, stop in next door and grab a burger and some cheese curds at the A&W. Happy Hour is 3–5pm when drinks are half price. Or if you adventure down the road there's a great taco stand.

Your task is to find the treasure from the clues provided. Be sure and leave the treasure at the spot for the next person to find.

Progressive Dinner

The other night we had a great time. We participated in a "progressive dinner." Pick one place for an appetizer, another for the main entre and another for dessert. For a little more fun, choose places you have never been before.

---

[1] http://www.google.com/search?q=audrey+hepburn
[2] http://www.google.com/search?q=geocaching
[3] http://www.geocaching.com/

A Quiet Date

Have a quiet date. The point is to be able to talk and enjoy each other's company without the pressure of being somewhere or doing something. Examples:

- Talk a walk in the park
- Go and watch a little league baseball game
- Take the dog for a walk

Enjoy the simple pleasure of time spent with a good friend.

Look for a Shooting Star

The Leonids Meteor Shower[1] happens each year around November 17-18. Take a blanket, some hot chocolate and go watch the stars. There are meteor showers thoughout the year. The ones in winter tend to be better because the night comes earlier and lasts longer.

Double Date

Remember when you used to "double date" in school? Once we did a double-quintuplet date (ten couples all together) while dating in high school. We had fun, even when all the girls went to the powder room together.

While generally not as "romantic," a double date can still be a lot of fun. One idea is to go to a baseball game together. Baseball tickets are still reasonably priced. Enjoy cheering for the home team and stop for ice cream on the way home.

Visit an Art Museum or Gallery

I went on a business trip to get some training in Chicago. Unfortunately, my sweetie was not able to come so I had to spend my evenings alone in a strange

---

[1] http://www.serve.com/wh6ef/comets/meteors/showers/leonidsez.html

city. One of my friends had told me about the Art Institute of Chicago[1], so I decided to go see it one evening. I found out that on Tuesday admission is free thanks to the generous support of Ford Motor Company. What a great evening I spent there. From the "Art of Flight" exhibit to the ancient armor and the paintings. It was a really enjoyable time. I just wish my sweetie could have shared it with me.

Of course not everyone lives in Chicago, I know I don't. But most places have art galleries and museums. Colleges and universities often have art displays and even some traveling exhibits. Even one of the malls here in town had a traveling Titanic exhibit for a while. Another bonus is that you can often get in free or very cheap.

Go Fly a Kite

When it is nice and breezy, it is so nice to be able to get out and enjoy the weather. What better way, weather permitting, to enjoy a nice day then to get a kite up in the air? Its fun but not that difficult. Rather than buying a kite, consider building your own[2], they aren't that hard.

The Newlywed Game for Two

Ever see a game show called *The Newlywed Game*? The premise of the show was to get newlywed couples on the show and to see how well they really knew each other. First, all the husbands were taken off stage. The wives were then asked fill in the blank type questions. Next, the husbands are brought back in and asked the same questions. Points were awarded if both husband and wife answered in the same way. Then the wives would go off stage and the process was repeated.

Modifying the game somewhat, here is an idea for a bunch of date nights (see page 77). Get two jars, one for restaurants and one for activities. On a slip of paper write the name of a restaurant where you like to eat. Make sure it is in your price range for a regular date. Put the slip of paper in the jar. Repeat as many times as you can think of places you like to eat. It would be good to

---

[1] http://www.artic.edu/aic/
[2] http://www.skratch-pad.com/kites/make.html

set a dollar limit before hand so you don't end up putting in restaurants that you can't afford except on special occasions. Have your spouse do likewise, but don't show each other what you have written. Consider only putting in equal numbers of papers. That is, you should both have the same numbers of papers added to the jar.

Do the same thing with the activities. Again, don't put things that are out of your price range or are not always available; a dollar limit is also a good idea here. For example, putting "see a movie" is ok but "go to the home show next week" is not ok. You will see why in a minute.

Now, on date night, reach in a grab one paper from the restaurant jar and one from the activity jar. Go and do whatever is written on the papers. This way you will end up doing stuff you each like to do, and getting to know more about each other in the process. Once a paper has been withdrawn, it can't be put back in until the jar is empty. That way you don't end up doing the same thing over again and miss doing some of the other things.

As you can see, it will take many dates over a long period of time to get through all the papers in both jars. That is why you can't include activities or meals that need to be done within a certain time frame.

Its also ok to just use one jar for a given date night. If you aren't going out to eat and just want to do an activity, that is just fine. The point is: a) to have regular dates, b) to do things on dates that each of you enjoy, and c) to break out of the "dinner-and-a-movie" mold. Just like in the newlywed game, you might find out some things about your sweetheart that you never knew before.

2–for–1 Dating

If you are like us, you get coupons in the mail, in the newspaper and even on the receipt at the grocery store. You can even buy a books of discount coupons or a coupon card from the kids in the neighborhood as part of a fund raiser. The problem we have is that we don't usually get the value out of it because we forget about even having the coupons over the course of a year.

Here is an idea: when you get coupons go through them and add the ones you are interested in into the date idea jar (see page 83). Then, when you draw out the coupon, not only will you have a good date idea, you will get a discount at it as well.

Getting Away From Everything

Every now and again, my sweetie and I like to get away. Our most recent get-away was at home. The kids went to stay with grandma and grandpa for a few days.

Re-dating

When you were courting and dating, you probably had some dates you still remember fondly. It may have been the night he proposed, or maybe she proposed. Maybe it was some other special time that was really meaningful in your relationship. Whatever it is, it will be unique to the two of you. Two couples can do the same thing, yet have very different experiences. Pick one special date from your own time courting.

Now that you have one in mind, re-do that date. For example, if it was when he popped the question, go back to the same place and do the same things, except popping the question as it is a one time only thing. By being in the same environment you will be surprised at how much more you remember about that special date.

If you have kids, take them along. Let them see how their goofy parents used to date and what you did for fun. Lots of things change, but people are still people. It will give your kids a positive example of what healthy dating should be.

How to Keep a Date from Bombing

Recently, we were watching an episode of a show we like to watch together called "Numbers". Its a television series about a math genius who helps his FBI brother solve tough cases by using math. I know, it sounds boring, but it really is a fun show.

During this last episode, the math genius finally worked up the nerve to ask out the girl he likes. They spent the first part of the date discussing mathematics but decide to talk about something else instead. At this point the conversation dries up because they have nothing else in common. The date ends up bombing due to a lack of anything to say to each other.

Later he asks what he could have done differently. I was tempted to shout the answer at the TV. However, through years of experience, I have determined that the characters in television shows rarely listen, no matter how loud I yell. Instead, I'll write my thoughts here.

Dating is as important in marriage as it is in courtship. What to do on a date is very important. For some strange reason, dinner and a movie is the "default date paradigm." Often, when we think about going on a date, its "what's playing?" While there is nothing wrong with dinner and a movie, there is very little right about it.

First, dinner. If you don't have much to say to each other, dinner can be long, painful and boring. Then, the movie. You sit next to each other not able to really interact. The movie ends and you can spend a few minutes talking about it, then that is that.

Rather, when considering a date consider having a shared experience. What is a shared experience? A shared experience is spending time together outside the comfort zone. Dinner and a movie is dead center in the comfort zone. Move outside the zone and create a memory.

Some ideas include:

- swimming
- dancing
- hiking or talking a walk
- bowling
- air hockey
- visiting an amusement park

It doesn't need to cost a lot or anything at all.

What would I tell the socially inept math genius? Do something physical and fun so you can have fun while you are being together. This does two things. First, it makes the current date a success, Second, it gives you something in common to talk about on the next date.

So keep dating, but do it outside the comfort zone. Dinner and a movie is good every so often, but only after you have had some shared experiences to keep the conversation going.

Free Concerts

My son needed to attend a concert and report on it for his band class. As we were looking around for possibilities, we found a free concert[1] at the local university. I and the oldest two kids went. Unfortunately, my sweetie was not able to attend.

This concert was unlike any other I have ever attended and it was way outside the realm of experience for my kids. The concert series consists of "experimental" music. There was percussion solo that was just incredible. Following this was a piano and flute duet which was interesting. The best way to describe it would be: "What would a flute sound like if it was alive and trying to get away while it was being played?" The musician seemed to be chasing his flute around the stage. My daughter had to cover her mouth to keep from laughing out loud while my son sat there with a quizzical look on his face. I had tears in my eyes from trying not to laugh at both the performance on stage and the reaction of my kids.

There was also a piano solo. On occasion, the pianist would slam down a hand or even his entire forearm onto the piano keys. My kids said "Mom gets mad at us when we do that." And they are right. Yet here we have a concert that involves playing a piano in just that sort of way.

When we got home, the kids spent quite some time telling their mother all about the concert. It will be something we will talk and laugh about for some time to come.

For an interesting evening, try a free concert at the local university or community arts council. You may like it or not, but it may be something different than you have experienced before. You can find them on the univeristy website, by checking your local paper, or checking at your local library.

The Importance of Being Earnest

In *The Importance of Being Earnest*, one of the characters quips: "The very essence of romance is uncertainty."

---

[1] http://carltonvickers.com/website/EVENTS.htm

What a wonderfully succinct way to sum up what romance is. The corollary is that what kills romance is a lack of uncertainty. Romance requires surprise, suspense and breaking out of the box. This is even more true after years of marriage than it was while dating.

The Importance of Being Earnest is a wonderful date night at home movie. A delightful romantic comedy which both husband and wife can enjoy.

Sharing a Sundae

Remember when you were a kid and your parents were trying to teach you to share? Or when you were trying to teach your own children to share?

Sharing an important aspect of human relations, especially romantic ones. One of the most romantic things to share is food. One of the most romantic moments in Disney's *Lady and the Tramp* is when they are sharing some spaghetti noodles. Each is eating at one end of the noodle until they meet together in the middle for a kiss.

When was the last time you shared a sundae? For some reason the ice cream and yummy toppings are just right for sharing. For an inexpensive and fun date, go to the ice cream parlor and order one sundae and two spoons.

Do You Believe in Reincarnation?

The April 2, 2006 *Hi and Lois*[1] is excellent. It shows the parents watching as a teenager leaves on a date. They then remember their dating for several panels. The last two panels:

> Wife: Seems like a different lifetime.
> Husband: Do you believe in reincarnation?
> Wife: Are you asking me out?
> Husband: Is that a "yes?"

I guess I really relate to the feeling that our courtship was a different lifetime ago. Bring that part of your relationship back to life. Ask that wonderful person you married on a date. The dating opportunities are abundant. If nothing else, go for a walk in the park. The point is not to spend money, but to spend time on each other.

---

[1] http://seattlepi.nwsource.com/fun/hi.asp

Valentines

Scavenger Hunt

Do you remember scavenger hunts? You a given a list of obscure items and tasks to perform. Of course, the trick is to not spend any money. A modified scavenger hunt is a great way to make Valentine's Day more memorable. It can be fun for your sweetie.

Prepare a bunch of gifts. Each gift contains a note leading to the next gift. Each gift includes a task to perform as well as directions to the next gift in the chain. The final note leads to where you are waiting.

The first note might say "Drop the kids off at Grandma's house." Then, when sweetie reaches Grandma's house, there is another gift with a note that says, "Go to friend's house". Friend then gives sweetheart desert and another note. Continue on with several steps. The last note will direct your sweetie to where you are waiting. This could be a restaurant or back home for a candlelight dinner for two.

Bouquets

Ok people listen up. What's it going to be this year? Are you going to do something memorable or will it be February 13th and you still haven't done anything? Decide early or the decision will be made for you. Here's an idea for the husbands, make her a dozen origami rose buds[1], mount them on green pipe cleaner and present them to her on the day. Before you fold each rose bud, write an action on the paper. Make it something like "make me laugh," "tell me a story," "kiss me so I see fireworks," "do the dishes," "cook dinner" or "rub my feet." Then attach a note stating that she should open a bud a day for the next twelve days and you will fulfill what ever the rose says.

Be sure that each action is simple enough that you can do it on any given night. You could also put a number on each rose bud and have her open specific roses on specific days. Then you can have the action planned for each rose. In that way you could include things like "go with me to see [movie title]." You would then get tickets, arrange for the babysitter and everything else so you can both go see the movie.

---

[1] http://www.bloom4ever.com/HowToFold.htm

Note guys, these roses are not simple to fold. You better give yourself some time to practice. Also, spend a little on some nice origami paper. Of course you can include the kids. They can help with folding the roses, presenting the bouquet and fulfilling the actions.

Loveland Valentine Program

Each year since 1946, the city of Loveland, Colorado[1] sets up a Valentine re-mailer. From their web-site:

> To have your valentines re-mailed, enclose your pre-stamped, pre-addressed Valentines with return address in a large 1st class envelope to: Postmaster Attn: Valentines Loveland, CO 80538-9998

What is a re-mailer? A re-mailer for snail-mail is the equivalent of a mail forwarder for e-mail. You get your valentines card, fill it out, put it in an envelope, address and stamp it. But do not mail it yet. Now get a larger envelope, address it to the address above with your return address. Put a stamp on it and put your valentine in this envelope. Seal it and send it to Loveland, Colorado. When they get it, they will "lovingly hand-stamp a special cachet with a message of love from Loveland on each valentine card received."

They will then send your valentine card to your sweetie. Have each of the kids send a valentine to your sweetie this way or send your kids a valentine. Everyone loves to get valentines in the mail.

There are other remailers as well:

> Cupid's Mailbox PO Box 201 Valentine, NE 69201

> Claire Langevin Postmaster Saint-Valentin Post Office, SAINT-VALENTIN QC J0J 2E0, Canada

> Love, Saskatchewan S0J 1P0, Canada

Valentine's Anti-Gift

I got my wife an early Valentine's present one year. It was a solid milk chocolate fish with packaging that looks like its ready to to be mounted on the wall. The name of the candy is "You're a keeper." She laughed and then went to show off

---

[1] http://www.loveland.org/events.asp?page=valentine_program

her fish to her friends, who also laughed. My kids thought it was the funniest thing ever. Although I didn't buy it, at the mall I saw a chocolate nose on a stick that said something like "If I hadn't picked you, nobody **knows** what I would have done!."

Having already given her a fish, I thought a nose might be too much. Valentine's tends to be a serious holiday with lots of romantic and expensive shows of affection. So a good gag gift is unexpected and is therefore more effective. Your sweetie will appreciate a good laugh, along with whatever romantic ideas you have. I will pass along to you my wife's advice to me, through the laughter: "This had better not be my whole Valentine's!"

Singing Telegram

My sweetie was in the hospital for Valentine's Day one year. Not how one would choose to spend the day most of the time, but those things happen. I also had a friend in a barbershop choir and they were raising money by doing singing telegrams. So, I paid him and he brought his barbershop quartet to my sweetheart's hospital room and sang a couple of songs for her and gave her a rose. Even now, several years later, she still talks about how wonderful it was. Of course all the nurses stopped to listen and enjoy. The other people on the hospital floor, when they saw my sweetie, told her how nice it was and how lucky she was to have such a thoughtful husband. When I arranged it, it never occurred to me how it would affect the other people in the hospital. She just beamed when people told her how sweet I was.

The point of this story is two-fold. First, when presented with an unexpected situation, come up with an unexpected way to show your sweetie how much you care. Second, it is more memorable if there are others to share in the fun.

Last Minute Flowers

Do you need a last minute Valentine's Day gift? Some of you, or maybe lots of you will be giving flowers this Valentine's Day. Flowers are an appropriate Valentine's gift for your sweetheart. The problem with flowers is that, while romantic, they are a bit common place. What can be done to make flowers more exciting?

Most of the time when you give flowers, you include a little note. Instead of the note, include something else that is small and paper. You could include movie or play tickets, a gift certificate or coupon to be used at a favorite restaurant with a note asking them to go out with you. As always, it's not the amount you spend, but the thought you put into it. As an example, if getting movie tickets, get them for that movie your sweetie has been wanting to see but you have been not enthusiastic about.

Who was Saint Valentine?

Who was Saint Valentine and why is he causing an uproar every year?

According to the *Catholic Encyclopedia's* entry on St. Valentine's Day[1] the reason for having St. Valentine's on February 14th is:

> The popular customs associated with Saint Valentine's Day undoubtedly had their origin in a conventional belief generally received in England and France during the Middle Ages, that on 14 February, i.e. half way through the second month of the year, the birds began to pair. Thus in Chaucer's Parliament of Foules we read: "For this was sent on Seynt Valentyne's day When every foul cometh ther to choose his mate." For this reason the day was looked upon as specially consecrated to lovers and as a proper occasion for writing love letters and sending lovers' tokens.

It seems that St. Valentine was a real person. From *Catholic Online's*St. Valentine[2] page:

> Since he was caught marrying Christian couples and aiding any Christians who were being persecuted under Emperor Claudius in Rome [when helping them was considered a crime], Valentinus was arrested and imprisoned. Claudius took a liking to this prisoner—until Valentinus made a strategic error: he tried to convert the Emperor—whereupon this priest was condemned to death. He was beaten with clubs and stoned; when that didn't do it, he was beheaded outside the Flaminian Gate [circa AD 269].

The article then goes on to state that he is the patron saint of affianced couples, bee keepers, engaged couples, epilepsy, fainting, greetings, happy marriages, love, lovers, plague, travellers, young people. He is represented in pictures with birds and roses.

---

[1] http://www.newadvent.org/cathen/15254a.htm
[2] http://www.catholic.org/saints/saint.php?saint_id=159

It seems that St. Valentine suffered martyrdom on February 14th and thus his name was associated with that day. Have a happy Valentine's Day.

Another Simple Gift Idea

One year my sweetheart gave me a large Mylar heart-shaped balloon that plays "You're the one that I want" when you tap it. The kids love it!

Oriental Trading Company

Valentine's is a great time of year. Romance is in the air and there are lots of romantic ideas about for married couples. One thing you might not have thought of, this is also a great time of year to replenish or start your spontaneity kit (see page 66). This kit is a collection of simple things that will allow you to do something special for your sweetie on a moment's notice. The few weeks before Valentine's is about the only time to stock up on heart shaped boxes, I-love-you stickers, and romantic candy. A fun and cheap place to find this sort of stuff at a great price is at Oriental Trading Company.

Candy Heart Image Generator

Here is a fun Valentine's idea for your sweetie. You can make your very own candy hearts[1] for your sweetheart. Of course, its just a picture (not actual candy so you can't eat it). Well, I guess you could eat it, but it wouldn't be very sweet.

Personalized Kisses

Like Fortune Cookies (see page 5), Hershey's Kisses contain a little message. And like fortune cookies, you can change out the little message for your own, more personal message.

While we were engaged, my sweetie gave me a pack of Hershey Kisses that she had personalized. It was so much fun to receive and to read all the fun,

---

[1] http://www.cryptogram.com/hearts/

thoughtful and goofy things she had written. We kept those little messages for a long time afterword.

The procedure is simple to follow, the trick is to be careful as you go. First, get a bag of kisses and *carefully* make a small opening in one end. Extract one kiss and practice opening it so that you can keep the foil nice for rewrapping. Also, keep the kisses paper to use a guide. Now eat that kiss.

Second, write on a sheet of paper a bunch of fun, thoughtful, complimentary, goofy little sayings. Each should be the size of the kiss paper you took out of the first kiss. Now cut out each paper but don't let them blow away.

Next, carefully take a kiss out of the bag and unwrap it. Replace the standard kiss paper with one of your own. Now, with equal care, rewrap the kiss and set it aside. Should you accidentally tear the foil, go ahead and eat the evidence. You don't have to eat the foil unless you like that sort of thing.

Once you have done all the kisses you are going to do, remove any remaining kisses from the bag and eat them. Now carefully insert your romantically enhanced kisses back into the bag and seal the opening.

Present the kisses to your sweetheart. If your sweetie is not very observant, you might need to drop a hint so that all your hard work does not go unnoticed.

"And the Most Important Trait in a Mate is . . . "

I saw this quote in the news:

> In the United States and Canada, humor was considered the most important trait by both men and women, getting sixty-three and seventy-three percent of the vote respectively.

I don't really put much stock into such studies, but when it proves my point, then its ok.

When did you and your sweetie laugh together last? Valentine's is a great time to laugh together. Like I told you before, I gave my sweetie a chocolate fish that says "You're a keeper." We still chuckle about it. Find some way to laugh together often.

Write a Love Letter

When was the last time you wrote your sweetheart a love letter? My sweetie mentioned that receiving a love letter would be a great Valentine's Day surprise.

I say I must agree with her. Writing a love letter can be a wonderful excerise that moves the writer out of the ordinary rut.

Not sure how to write a love letter? Not to fret, here are some great ideas to get you started, followed by places you can find even more information on the subject. Isn't the Internet wonderful?

- When stealing, steal from the best! Use freely from the bard[1], the lyrics to romantic love songs[2] and poems

Doubt thou the stars are fire; Doubt that the sun doth move; Doubt truth to be a liar; But never doubt I love.

- Hand written on specialty paper is nice (if your hand writing is not all that romance inspiring, consider having a professional calligrapher write your thoughts for you)
- Include compliments on all aspects of your sweetheart: physical characteristics, talents and accomplishments
- Express gratitude for the wonderful things your sweetie does
- Tell your sweetheart ways in which he/she makes you a better person
- Remember shared times together
- Include a little humor

Suggested reading:

- Love Letter Etiquette[3]
- Best Love Letters[4]

A final quote:
If I know what love is, it is because of you.

Flowers

I know, I know.

---

[1] http://shakespeare.about.com/cs/generalsites/a/weddingreadings.htm
[2] http://www.lyrics007.com/Queen%20Lyrics/You%27re%20My%20Best%20Friend%20Lyrics.html
[3] http://www.cyberparent.com/love/loveletter.htm
[4] http://honeymoons.about.com/cs/lvlettermain/

There is nothing unique about giving flowers for Valentine's Day. It is a standard gift to give. Floral arrangements cost a lot of money and die after a few days. The cost problem is even more pronounced at this time of year.

However, you can add a twist to the whole flower giving clique. It is possible to give flowers and be non-boring as well. You can even save a few bucks in the process.

First, consider giving some different arrangements (see page 63). Add something to the flowers, like chocolate covered strawberries. Maybe include the flowers in a scavenger hunt. Deliver the flowers to your sweetheart's place of work. Use the flowers as dressing on the "real gift," such as a love letter.

Now cost. My sweetheart mentioned that Costco has 25 long stemmed roses with a vase for under $50.00. Shop around and look at non-traditional source like warehouse places. Also many times you can find discounts on the Internet.

Not Exactly What I Was Expecting

I have to admit that even I don't think of Home Depot for Valentine's Day. Yet, there on their front page[1] is a big Valentine's Day banner. I had to click on it. You know what, I was a bit surprised.

Did you know that you can order roses from Home Depot? Me neither. But I guess you can. They even throw in a free vase. Who knew?

Of course you can get your sweetie that romantic laser level kit. Or maybe the screwdriver. They do have a heart-shaped waffle maker. That would be fun.

Last Minute Ideas

Yup, you can still get roses delivered.

Don't forget that a love letter is still a great last minute gift. Put it on some nice paper for added impact.

Surprise your sweetie by inviting your sweetheart to a long lunch. It makes for a fun and inexpensive way to celebrate.

Most book stores sell "love coupons." They are a great way to let your sweetheart know you care. The coupons include things like "one night off from chores" or "go out to eat, your choice of restaurant." You get the idea.

---

[1] http://www.homedepot.com/

Of course most stores have valentines candy, flowers and cards. I found some on sale yesterday.

I'm in Hot Water Today

The day after Valentine's Day I was in hot water with my wife. You guessed it, it's all over my Valentine's gift to her. In spite of my planning and scheming, Valentine's Day did not go off quite as planned.

The story starts on the Sunday before. We came home from church to the sound of an alarm blaring through the house. Due to a high water table in the area, we have water alarms on the floor in case water starts to seep into the basement. One of these alarms was squealing for all its worth. The problem is that they are so high pitched, you can't readily tell where its coming from. So we start hunting around the basement trying to find the water. No water in the usual places. Finally, we see the water heater has a small leak. It is thirteen years old and was probably due to be replaced soon anyway.

There go all my big, just-got-my-tax-refund, plans. This year my wife is getting a hot water heater for Valentine's Day. Never was there a more romantic gift given. I also got her the solid chocolate fish.

The evening before Valentine's Day was spent installing this most romantic of gifts. The plan was to be able to enjoy a nice hot shower in the morning to celebrate the new water heater. That night before going to bed, she checks and sure enough there is plenty of hot water coming from the tap.

Valentine's Day morning: something has happened overnight. There is no longer any hot water. Its not that the water is not hot, its that there is no water coming out of the hot water tap at all. When the hot water is turned on, a whole lot of nothing comes out of the tap. The cold water comes out ok, and very cold.

Oh, this was not a good omen. A cold shower is not how I was wanting to start Valentine's Day. My poor son had to wash his hair in the sink using cold water. Brrrrrr.

So I stayed home from work to get the hot water fixed. Finally, after a while I get it all figured out and the hot water is restored. I will plead the fifth on the reason it wasn't working. Suffice it to say the installation instructions could have been more clear on a couple of minor points.

Peace and harmony were restored. My sweetie was able to enjoy a nice hot shower. Something we daily take for granted but are more grateful for today.

Now we found ourselves alone as the kids were all off to school. This does not happen very often and we decided to take advantage by spending some time together running a few simple errands.

Our first errand was to get rid of the old hot water heater. At the local refuse dump they have a place to drop off scrap metal to be recycled. So we ran down to the dump, my sweetie paid the three dollars to get in and I threw the old hot water heater on the pile.

As I got back into the truck, I realized what I had done. My wife's Valentine's Day had consisted of:

- A malfunctioning hot water heater
- A solid chocolate fish that says "You're a keeper"
- A trip to the dump, where she had to pay

As I pointed this out to my sweetheart, we both broke into laughter until tears came from our eyes. She was thinking of how she could brag to her friends about how romantic the day had been. This was one of those Valentine's Days we will remember and enjoy laughing about for many years to come.

So that is how I got into hot water on Valentine's Day. I don't know how I'll be able to outdo myself next year, but maybe I'll think of something.

The Twinkie in My Brown Bag of Life

A very clever blogger shared a great notion of a simple, inexpensive and romantic Valentine's gift. Over at Cleverly Blogged[1] we read:

> I once sent [my sweetie] a card that said: *"You are the twinkie in my brown bag lunch of life."*
> She thought that was a very sweet thing for me to have said. So from time to time I'll buy her a twinkie as a reminder that she still is the twinkie in my brown bag lunch of life.

Good work and a good example for us all.

---

[1] http://blog.cleverly.com/

Christmas and Other Holidays

An Un-special Occasion Card

People usually think of greetings cards only for "special" occassions like birthdays, Valentine's Day and Christmas. Special life events like births, deaths, and graduations are also remembered with a greeting card. For the rest of the year, we tend to forget about these little beauties.

Next time you are at the store, look at the greetings cards. Not only are there cards for every sort of special occassion, there are also a variety of "friendship," "romance" and "thank you" cards.

Find one of these cards. If in doubt, you can't go wrong with a thank you card. Wait until you have no reason whatsoever to send it. Hand write a short message of love and gratitude. Hand address the envelope then stamp and mail it. Remember: SWAK

25 Days of Thanksgiving

On November 1 place an empty cornucopia somewhere conspicuous in the house (maybe on the kitchen table as a centerpiece, maybe in the living room on a coffee table). If you have little ones, keep it out of their reach. Then get a pad of multi-colored paper that is convenient to the cornucopia. From November 1 until Thanksgiving, pay attention to the things your spouse does for you and your family.

When you notice something, write it on a piece of the colored paper. Then fold the note over and place in the cornucopia. Come Thanksgiving, read the notes of gratitude together as a family. A couple of rules:

1. No fair peeking

2. Put at least one in everyday

3. Don't peek at the notes until Thanksgiving day

4. Make each note specific (Bad note: laundry; Good note: On November 1st it was so nice to have an ironed shirt to wear to meet the boss)

5. No peeking until Thanksgiving

This could be a great way to include the entire family—everyone could participate by including notes of gratitude for the entire family.

Mistletoe

What better tradition is there than being expected to kiss your sweetie for no other reason than just standing in the right spot? Add mistletoe to your Christmas decorations. Be sure to put it somewhere where you will often be together. Even better, get two, one for the bedroom and one for the kitchen (or wherever you often meet).

Now to the good part, the kissing. What sort of kiss should you do under the mistletoe? As many sorts as you can think of. One time give her a peck on the cheek. Next time, give her a toe-curling whopper. Be sure to mix it up with kisses to her cheeks, lips, nose, hands, neck, etc. Whatever you do, do not become predictable. Keep her guessing how she is going to be kissed next. Spice up your repertory by throwing butterfly kisses and Eskimo kisses into the mix for a greater variety of surprises.

Also, add various other aspects to the kiss. Perform one kiss while holding hands. Do another in a full bear hug. Try giving her a love-pat or not touching her at all. Sometimes whisper a sweet nothing in her ear or sneak a love note into her hand or pocket. Take your time and linger sometimes. Other times, make it quick, almost an ambush.

Most important: Always smile. Let her see in your countenance how you much you enjoy kissing her.

What about the kids? It is good for kids to both be kissed and to see their parents kissing. For example, our youngest has a good friend whose parents were getting divorced. It was surprising to realize how much my child has been affected by that divorce and how she worries about my wife and I getting a divorce. With so many marriages dissolving before your children's eyes, your kids need to have confidence in the stability of your family. Give them that confidence by letting them see you kiss and otherwise flirt with your sweetie. It really helps them to feel more confident in themselves when they can feel secure about the stability of their family.

Bonus: One time you will give her a peck on the cheek and she will grab you and give you a fireworks kiss. Congratulation! You did it right.

Gifts with Meaning

Turn a simple gift into a more meaningful and memorable gift experience. Instead of getting a single gift, get several smaller gifts. Make the gifts things that your sweetie really could use. Often, the gifts we need aren't that romantic. To give the gift a romantic touch, include a small note with the gift.

For example, if the gift is long johns then the note might say "because your smile gives me the warm-fuzzies." I think you have the idea. Now wrap each small gift individually with the accompanying note, then place all the wrapped small gifts into a larger box and wrap it. By putting a little extra effort and creativity into your gifts, you can turn a mundane item into a romantic experience for both of you.

Involve the children, have each kid contribute a gift and a note into the box. They will love to watch as the gifts are opened and appreciated. If one or more of the gifts are not "kid appropriate," create two boxes. One will have the stuff the kids included and can be opened with the whole family. The other box can include the other, more personal gifts to be opened in private.

Free Electronic Greeting Cards

You can send an electronic greeting card to your sweetheart for free. Just go to Hallmark[1] and press the Free E-Cards link. Look for it in the second column under the picture. The column header is "our products."

I've sent a couple of these to people and they are fun. They have all sorts of cards. It is a lot of fun to look at all cards. Also, the cards can be personalized so that you can add your own romantic message.

Even though you have to enter both your email and your sweetie's email, I have not noticed any increase in spam. Hallmark seems to not be collecting these for mass-marketing purposes. The other slight drawback is that the card requires Flash to read, but that shouldn't be a problem unless the recipient uses an older web browser.

---

[1] http://www.hallmark.com/

Burma Shave Signs

Have you ever heard of Burma Shave[1]? They sold shaving cream from the '20s to the '60s, which is not very interesting in itself. Lots of companies sell shaving cream. What made Burma Shave different was the advertising. Even today, forty years after the last ad, people still know Burma Shave ads.

A Burma Shave ad consisted of a 4 line verse like:

- *If your peach*
- *keeps out of reach*
- *better practice*
- *what we preach*

Each line of the verse was placed on a large poster and staked into the ground along the road. As a driver was driving down the road, they would read one line. Then a short while later, the next sign, then the next and finally the last. There was then a fifth sign with the Burma Shave logo. The first sign got your attention but then you had to wait for the whole verse.

What has this to do with romance? Anticipation. We all love a sense of anticipation. Create the anticipation with a small verse of your own. Write four lines of love and gratitude to your sweetie. Place each line on a poster. Then create a last poster that says "[sweetie's name, I love you, [your name]."

You can either mount the posters on the drive up to your house where your sweetheart will see them on the way home or you can mount them throughout the house, starting at the door where your sweetie will enter the house.

This can be used on a special day, like a birthday or as a just because "I Love You" and wanted you to know it.

You can search Google for more Burma Shave info.

April Fool's Day

Ok, most of us think of Valentines (see page 92) when we think of romantic holidays. But April Fool's Day day can also be romantic, with just a little thought.

---

[1] http://frogcircus.org/burmashave/

The essence of a romantic April Fool's prank is to surprise your sweetie. Instead of pulling a practical joke, pull an indirection instead. A couple of ideas:

- Remove the light bulb from the bedroom and call sweetie back to fix it. Use your imagination of what to do in the dark.
- Bring take out dinner home and put it in the oven. Tell sweetie you slaved all day making their favorite. Bring out the dinner, still in the take out boxes.
- Tell sweetie the power is out and have a cold dinner by candlelight.
- A romantic gag gift
- Get a romantic card or a suggestive card and write April Fools on the envelope and put "Since we have some time alone, let's have lunch at _____" on the inside of the card. Drive somewhere within walking distance of nice restaurant. Call sweetie and say the car broke down and that you need a ride. Make sure sweetie finds the card. Have lunch.
- If you are home during the day and sweetie can get away from work, have a mock emergency at home.

Turn the practical joke into a romantic gesture.

Sweetie Appreciation Week

Declare some week to be "Sweetie Appreciation Week." Mark it on your calendar a couple of weeks in the future so that the anticipation can build. Then, each day during the week do something to show that you appreciate your sweetheart. Mine would look like:

- Monday: Footrub
- Tuesday: A note of appreciation
- Wednesday: Her favorite treat
- Thursday: One hour of "sweetie" time
- Friday: Her favorite meal and video

Also send a romantic card in the mail on Monday so your sweetie will get it at some random time during the week.

Cinco de Mayo

A friend of mine has dual citizenship in the U.S. and in Canada. This lucky dog gets to celebrate twice as many holidays as I do. He has two Thanksgiving feasts, although it takes me about a year to recover from just the one. The Canadians also have extra holidays[1] like Boxing Day, Easter Monday and Canada Day. Just because my friend celebrates the Canadian holidays, does that make him a poor citizen of the United States of America? No, of course not. Especially when I get to celebrate with him.

Looking south instead of north we see Cinco de Mayo, which is a big celebration in Mexican history. Some facts about Cinco de Mayo[2]:

- It is **not** Mexican independence day (which is actually September 16)
- It celebrates the defeat of a larger, better equipped French army by a smaller army of Mexicans in the state of Puebla
- During the American Civil War, Napoleon tried to invade Mexico and add it to his empire
- The US helped out the Mexicans, once the Civil War was over

What better excuse for a fiesta (see page 61) than to join in with the celebrations of our neighbor to the south. Some ways of celebration Cinco de Mayo include:

- Have Mexican food for dinner (many Mexican restaurants celebrate this day)
- Go to a Cinco de Mayo festival in your community
- Play some Mexican games[3]
- Watch the Mask of Zorro (ok, it doesn't really have anything to do with Cinco de Mayo, but it is still fun!)

Feliz Cinco de Mayo!

---

[1] http://www.pch.gc.ca/progs/cpsc-ccsp/jfa-ha/index_e.cfm
[2] http://www.mexonline.com/cinco.htm
[3] http://www.kidsdomain.com/holiday/cinco/party.html

Recorded Message

As discussed previously, a personalized message (see page 2) means so much more than just saying it. Hand written notes mean more than email. Why? Its the difference between a work of art and a product off the assembly line. The work of art is one of a kind. It is unique and there will never be another one like it. Same with your hand written note. Same with your sweetie.

My wife and I came across some audio tapes we had. One I had recorded and sent to her. The family had so much fun listening to them. It had been a lot of years and we had forgotten what was even on them.

Why not make an audio tape or CD for your sweetie? Rather than trying to sit down and recording a whole hour, record it in little sound bites over two or three weeks. Include on it funny things (see page 10) that have happened, things your sweetie has done that you appreciated (see page 9), little things you are planning on doing (see page 59), and how much you love your sweetheart (see page 10). Once it is done, wrap it up and give it to your sweetie.

Mother's Day

Mother's Day, they say, is a made up holiday. Just an excuse for the flower companies and greeting card companies to make money during an off season of the year. Well, we here at FerociousFlirting.com[1] feel that made up holidays (see page 61) are just fine. Particularly holidays dedicated to how much we love and appreciate our sweethearts.

My mother is not perfect, although just about. She was the perfectest mother I ever had. She protected me, even when I didn't think I needed protection. She tried to guide my chosen career in life, but for the life of me I can't figure out why she wanted me to be a physicist. Maybe I'll ask her later today. However, she did not stand in the way of me becoming a professional geek (software engineer). Mother tried to make sure I married the "right" girl and when I found my own right girl to marry, she loved her too.

My wife is perfect for me. As I watch her sacrifice herself for her children, I finally understand what my own mother sacrificed for me and my siblings. The

---

[1] http://www.ferociousflirting.com/

worries and the pain of watching kids commit follies and suffering the consequences. The joy of sharing in the little triumphs: kicking a goal, scoring a hundred on a test, making the orchestra, or drawing a beautiful horse.

My sweetheart is one of those people who can doing anything exceptionally well. When she decides to do something, not only does it get done, it gets done superbly. She is also amply blessed with so many talents. She sings, dances, plays flute, draws, sews, teaches. When ever she asks me to do some task around the house, its not because she can't do it better than I can, because she can.

Mom, I love and appreciate all that you have done for me and my family.

Sweetie, thanks for blessing my life by sharing your life with me. I love you.

Sharing your Ancestors

On Memorial Day we make it a point to visit graves of both my family and that of my sweetie. I have started taking pictures of the headstones, but I am into genealogy[1] that way. One fun part of genealogy is meeting distant relatives over the internet.

This year, as you visit the cemetery, take your digital camera along. Take nice pictures of the headstones. When you get back home, go to Find A Grave[2] and add your ancestors and those of your sweetheart. They allow you to include pictures so you can upload those pictures you took. It is a great way to honor and remember.

Memorial Day

Many people have sacrificed much—even their lives—for us. Many are in harms way today doing the same. Take a moment to look outside your own relationship and remember and honor those who have defended us and who are now defending us. Our prayers are with you all.

---

[1] http://m0smith.freeshell.org/JosephAnthonyThomas/
[2] http://www.findagrave.com/

Father's Day Shopping

This year Father's Day and my birthday fall within a few weeks of each other. I guess they always do, funny how that works out. Anyway, my sweetie has started asking "what do you want for Father's Day and your birthday?" My standard answer has been either "nothing" or "I've already got what I want" and give her a big kiss.

The real problem has been that I never remember what it is I want. So this year I have been keeping notes. There are a couple of ways of keeping notes (see page 1):

- On a piece of paper. Old fashioned, but it still works! When you think of something you want, just find your paper and write it down
- In a PDA. This is a bit more convenient if you already have one you carry with you
- Camera phone. When you see something you like, email yourself a picture of it and keep it in a special folder
- Use Amazon's Wish List I like this one because then I can easily share it with anyone

When people ask what you want, they really want to know. Give them some choices. Maybe they won't get you exactly what you wanted, but it still might give them some good ideas of what sorts of things you are interested in. Remember that people change (see page 10) and what a person wants may change over time.

Flag Day

An essential part of keeping the fire going in a relationship is to see yourself as part of a greater whole. The notion of "what's in it for me" gives way to "what can I do for the marriage" and then "what's in it for us." The marriage should be fulfilling to both parties.

We are all also part of a community, state, and country. By flying the flag and taking a moment to ponder all the people who have worked and suffered and died, you can feel part of the greater whole.

Look outside your own perspective.

Father's Day Breakfast

My wife and I don't see much of each other in the mornings. On the weekdays she gets up and goes for a walk. By the time she gets back, I have already left for work. To top it off, neither of us are morning people so even if we do see each other first thing in the morning, its not all that romantic. Just a grunt good morning. Although she would like to make my breakfast, it just isn't possible and I am perfectly capable of feeding myself.

Sundays are even worse. My responsibilities at church require me to be there by 6:30 am, while my wife doesn't even need to get up until I have been gone for a couple of hours. I do not begrudge her this extra sleep as she gets to wrangle the kids and get them ready for church. She deserves some extra rest. Again, I end up getting my own breakfast.

On Father's Day my wife made me a very special breakfast. The food itself was standard breakfast fare. What made it special is that she got up at 5:45am to get it ready for me. This was a big sacrifice on her part and it meant a lot to me.

Fireworks

Fireworks are great fun and can make for a cheap or even free date. Most cities have fireworks for free. Take some drinks and munchies, go early and find your spot, lay out a blanket or lawn chairs and wait for the show to start.

Another fun idea is to make a double header of it. Go to a baseball game where they are having fireworks afterwards. It is a lot of fun to cheer on the home team and then share the fireworks with 20,000 of your closest friends.

Of course the kids will like the fireworks as well.

Season to Fall in Love Again

In Season to Fall In Love (see page 75) I wrote about the wonders of fall. We often speak of spring as the season of love and it truly is. However, fall is also a season of love. It is harvest time, the time to reap what we have sown. A time of plenty and thanksgiving (see page 103). A time to prepare for winter.

Sow thoughtfulness to reap romance. Sow thankfulness to reap joy. Sow kindness to reap peace.

Favorite Halloween Movies

Here are a couple of my favorite movies to watch on Halloween. I do not go for the slasher movies.

The Nightmare Before Christmas: For those who never thought the Walt Disney Company would release a film in which Santa Claus is kidnapped and tortured, well, here it is! The full title is *Tim Burton's The Nightmare Before Christmas*, which should give you an idea of the tone of this stop-action animated musical / fantasy / horror / comedy.

Arsenic and Old Lace: Frank Capra made this film in 1941 before he went off to make films for America's war effort, but it wasn't released until 1944. Adapted from the hit play by Joseph Kesselring, this frantic black comedy shows Capra at his best as a master of mood and timing.

Ghostbusters: Dan Aykroyd and Harold Ramis wrote the script, but Bill Murray gets all the best lines and moments in this 1984 comedy directed by Ivan Reitman (Meatballs). The three comics, plus Ernie Hudson, play the New York City-based team that provides supernatural pest control, and Sigourney Weaver is the love interest possessed by an ancient demon. Reitman and company are full of original ideas about hobgoblins—who knew they could "slime" people with green plasma goo?—but hovering above the plot is Murray's patented ironic view of all the action. Still a lot of fun, and an obvious model for later sci-fi comedies such as Men in Black.

Veteran's Day

On this day when we honor veterans, let us also remember those who are in harm's way in service to their country. Previously I talked about sending a package to a soldier (see page 125). It would be a great way to honor and support those who are currently giving so much for their country.

In Flanders Fields

By: Lieutenant Colonel John McCrae, MD (1872–1918)

In Flanders fields the poppies blow
Between the crosses row on row,
That mark our place; and in the sky
The larks, still bravely singing, fly
Scarce heard amid the guns below.

We are the Dead. Short days ago
We lived, felt dawn, saw sunset glow,
Loved and were loved, and now we lie
In Flanders fields.

Take up our quarrel with the foe:
To you from failing hands we throw
The torch; be yours to hold it high.
If ye break faith with us who die
We shall not sleep, though poppies grow
In Flanders fields.

McCrae's "In Flanders Fields" remains to this day one of the most memorable war poems ever written. It is a lasting legacy of the terrible battle in the Ypres Salient[1] in the spring of 1915. (Lt. Col. McCrae served in the Canadian Army.)

Online Shopping Lists

Christmas[2] is coming, consider yourself warned. And yes, that radio station has been playing Christmas carols since Halloween. What are you going to get for your sweetheart this year?*Make a Note of It* (see page 1) talks about the importance of keeping a list of those things your sweetie has been wanting. There are a couple of online places to keep track of such lists.

Amazon.com has a "Wish List." It allows you to keep a list of all items available on Amazon. Of course, they also make it easy to buy those items from Amazon.

Froogle.com[3] also has a Wish List feature. Like the Amazon list, it allows you to create a list of products you are interested in. The Froogle list seems easier

---

[1] http://www.arlingtoncemetery.net/flanders.htm
[2] http://www.kosy.com/main.html
[3] http://froogle.google.com/

to share than Amazon's. Also, since it isn't pegged to a single supplier, it shows a price comparison of the product from various shops, which I like.

This Wish Lists can work two ways. First, you maintain a list of things you think your sweetie is interested in. Second, your sweetheart creates a list and shares it with you. That way you can remove some of the stress of Christmas shopping.

Black Friday

The day after Thanksgiving is not Boxing Day, its Black Friday. Its the day the stores hope to make piles of money. To encourage people to give them lots of money they do lots of crazy things like open early, have ridiculously low prices on certain items and otherwise attempt to become between me and my money.

This explains why the alarm went off at 4:10 A.M. on Friday morning. At this time I discovered another meaning for Black Friday—it was really, really dark. The sun was not due up for some time and here I was rushing to some store like an idiot with my dear sweetheart. I won't burden you with the rest of the tale: the lines, the driving, the cold, or the vast amount of money we gave to various establishments. No, you don't need all the gory details.

Wait! Isn't this supposed to be a romantic site? Believe or not, as we spent the morning promoting capitalism, we also improved our relationship. We had lots of time in lines to **talk undisturbed by children**. We moved **outside the comfort zone** (and into the cold). We have some funny war stories to tell, like the one guy... Oh sorry, back on topic. We were **working on common goals** . We have some **shared successes to celebrate** as well as some **near misses to commiserate**.

The point is, getting up early and spending a few hours with your sweetie is a great way to pass the time. However, we decided that no matter how good the sale, we are not going to any more 5:00 A.M. store openings; 6:00 A.M. is fine with us thank you very much. And a jug of hot cocoa will definitely be on the list.

Christmas on Temple Square

Christmas on Temple Square[1] is a wonderful opportunity for those of you in the Salt Lake area. Bundle up, check out the lights on temple square and enjoy a free program. Every city has some sort of display and even some neigborhoods put on light displays.

Romantic Christmas Tip: Building Anticipation

Did you get your sweetie something special for Christmas? Of course you did, or you better. Want to know how to make it even more fun? Use the same principle as the advent calendar.

An advent calendar is a way to count down the days left until Christmas. My wife made one that is just a blank wall hanging with twenty-four buttons on it. Each day a new element is added to one of the buttons. On Christmas it is a creche with baby Jesus, angels, animals and so on. Our kids love to add a new element each day. It helps to build the anticipation and excitement for the big day.

Use the same technique with your special gift you are giving your sweetie. Start leaving obscure clues and dropping obtuse hints about the nature of the gift. Your hints can include things like cost, size, and intended use. Be sure to only give one hint a day. Also, be sure that none of the hints individually—or all of the hints together—give it away.

Perhaps an example. Say you are giving your sweetie an iPod for Christmas. Your hints might include the following:

- Its smaller than a breadbox (classic size comparison)
- Its goes well with your skin tone (maybe jewelry or clothing)
- Its shiny (more jewelry)
- It will make everyone jealous
- It will help with your daily chores
- It will enhance your beautiful eyes (compliment)

---

[1] http://www.lds.org/calendar/

I think you get the idea. Leave each hint on a post-it note in an obvious place. By the time Christmas comes, your sweetie will really be feeling the anticipation.

Good Luck and have fun. Merry Christmas everyone.

Exulant Solstice to Everyone

December 21 is a great day to Create Your Own Holiday (see page 61). Winter Solstice makes the shortest day of the year, but it is also the longest night of the year. Do something sweet to surpise your sweetie today. I'm going to suggest avoiding candies and such though. We are on goodie overload at out house again this year.

Some ideas include:

- Send a Soltice Greeting eCard[1]
- Surprise them with flowers or other non-Christmasy surprise
- Have lunch together (see page 130)

Exulant Solstice to all.

Celebrate Pi Day

National Pi[2] Day is March 14th (3.14) festivities begin at 1:59. In honor of the occasion, I would suggest a surprise pie for your sweetie.

Also, remember, in spite of what they may have taught you in math πr^2 , pies are really round. (Say it out loud, Gracie.)

See the official PiDay.org[3] website.

Pot of Gold

St. Patricks Day is in March. For a surprise for your sweetie, get a pot and fill it with chocolate gold coins. Mix in with the gold coins some scraps of gold paper with the reasons you treasure your sweetie and your marriage.

---

[1] http://www.123greetings.com/cgi-bin/search/search.pl?words=solstice&fpage=HPsearch

[2] http://www.exploratorium.edu/learning_studio/pi/

[3] http://www.piday.org/

Family

Family Romance

Admit it, you think that children and romance don't mix. Most people think that way. Yet, as parents, we love our children very much. So why can't a romantic gesture include the whole family? Well, the answer is it can! Here is a simple example of how this can be accomplished:

Purchase a dozen roses. Give one or two to each child. Then have each child deliver their flowers and say somehting like "I know who mommy's boyfriend is." Send each child individually and wait a few minutes in between. Then lastly deliver the rest of the flowers yourself.

Kids need to see that their parents are in love. They enjoy being part of the surprise. Besides it is lots of fun too.

The Goal of Life

People like winners—they are fun to be around. We love to cheer for the winning team. Movies, books and sports all have examples of people putting it on the line. They step outside the ordinary to do something extrordinary. This sets them apart as someone special.

Today its time to get outside the comfort zone. Set yourself some goals to improve yourself. Need to get in better shape? Set a goal. Some skills you are lacking? Set a goal. Then share the goal with that special someone. Make plans with them to help you reach that goal. Then let them cheer you along the way. Share your successes and your diffuculties. As you reach your goals, you can be a winner. Remember everyone loves a winner.

100–100

We often hear that a marriage should be 50–50. Each partner should contribute half to the relationship. By implication, each partner would then withhold 50% from the relationship as well. Consider a football team. If each member of the team does his half best, would this team go very far?

A marriage is the ultimate team. Each member of the team needs to give it 100%. The husband needs to be 100% dedicated to the wife and the wife 100%

dedicated to her spouse and both need to be 100% dedicated to the marriage. Just as players on a football team need to be 100% dedicated to the team.

"Wait!" you say, "I can add. 100% + 100% = 200% How can a single person give 200%. That's just crazy talk." Welcome to the concept of synergy. By dedicating yourself completely to your spouse, and your spouse doing the same, you create synergy.

You are able to do more as a team than either of you can do alone. It is like in those war movies when one soldier says "I got your back." They then stand back to back and face the oncoming enemy. Each knows he doesn't need to worry about what's behind him as his partner has that under control.

In a marriage, each partner is responsible for certain tasks. On a football team there are different positions played by different people. Each needs to know what is expected of him and to trust the other team members to do their part as well. By guarding each other's back, you and your sweetie can remain 100% focused on the position you have to fill in the relationship knowing that you won't be blindsided because your partner has his postilion filled as well.

Hobbies

Most people have hobbies. Hobbies can include stamp collecting, bird watching, photography, fishing, crafting, knitting and so on. It might even be writing or following a particular football team. Whatever it is, your sweetie probably has one and you probably know what it is. If you don't know what your sweetie's hobby is, find out.

Just as likely, your sweetie does not have time to pursue that hobby. With the demands of marriage, kids, career and everything else which consumes our time, most of us have precious little time to pursue our own interests. Often, we feel guilty about spending time on doing "my thing." The result is those things aside and ignored for a long time.

Another common thing is that husband and wife do not share the same hobbies. He's into football and she likes gardening. This is another reason people put hobbies aside. What little free time people have, most would rather spend it with their spouse. It often ends up a decision of whether to spend time on the hobby or the spouse. Most people choose spouse.

As a special treat for your sweetie, you should enable them to enjoy both their hobby and your company. Lets take the case where your sweetie likes to watch the Rams play football but never seems to have time to sit and watch a game. Find out when the Rams are playing and arrange a "football date" at home. Make nachos or popcorn or whatever the favorite football treat is. Invite a couple of friends over to watch the game game on TV with you. The idea is to allow some guilt free time to enjoy both the game and your companionship.

This is just one example, but the same principle can work with any hobby. The idea is three-fold: first, remove the guilt associated with spending time on a hobby instead of something else; second, participate to some extent in the hobby so it can end up being "us time" as well as "my thing;" and third, do something to encourage the hobby (this can be making necessary arrangements or by buying something useful to the hobby).

Blackout

For a fun evening at home, have a pretend blackout. The idea is simple: just don't use anything that has to be plugged in to work. This includes: TV, computer, stereo, lights, oven, microwave, etc. Do leave the fridge running though. Use flash lights, lanterns, or whatever. Spend the time normally devoted to TV by talking, telling stories and playing games.

Note: be careful when using candles that they are not unattended. Also, do not use anything in the house that requires propane or kerosene. It can build up carbon monoxide.

Swimming

Swimming is great for couples. It feels good and is wonderful exercise. If you don't have access to a private pool, most communities have a nice public facility for a small cost. Spend some time laughing, splashing, swimming and just having fun while getting your heart rate up. If you have kids, all but the littlest can participate.

Cut a Rug

When was the last time you danced with your sweetie? If you are like most couples, you can't remember that far back. Tonight, clear a spot and find some music of varying tempos. It is as important to have some up-tempo music as well as the "bear hug" music. Then, spend a few minutes dancing with your sweetheart.

Dancing is great for your both your hearts—the physical one and the romantic one. For the physical heart, it is a wonderful aerobic activity that will get your heart rate up. It burns lots of calories and gets those endorphins going to make you feel good.

But don't forget the romantic heart. By the end of just a couple of dances you both will be smiling, laughing and really enjoy being with each other. Not only that, there is a lot of touching: hugs, holding hands, the "bump" and so on. No better recipe for romance was ever written.

What about the kids? Unless you have teenage sons, they will be jumping right in. Kids know a good time when they see it. You may have daughters standing on your feet or a son "dancing" without his even touching the ground. Its a great family "bonding" experience.

You say, "I am so self-conscious of my dancing." The best way to overcome that it to make a game of it. There are no set rules for dancing. Dancing only requires a willingness to try. Make up your own dances based on everyday stuff: the lawnmower, the dishwasher, etc. Just be sure to laugh at yourself.

Gift Idea: Your Story

Although it is marketed as a children's product, the IlluStory Book Kit can make a great romantic gift for your sweetie. The book is short—only allows for about twenty words per page. Some of the things you can do are:

- Make a book about how you met and fell in love
- Create a story with your sweetie as the hero (have your sweetheart do the things they have never been able to do)
- Create a family history album with each page being a different person from your family tree
- Make each page something you love about your sweetie
- Make the book together as a short joint auto-biography
- Use you imagination and create a book unique to you

The kids will love reading this book over and over again. It will be even more fun for them if at least one page includes them. No matter how silly it turns out, this book will become a family favorite.

Family Night

Each week have a Family Night[1].

What is Family Night?

Family Night is a special time set aside each week that brings family members together and strengthens their love for each other, helps them draw closer to Heavenly Father, and encourages them to live righteously.

How is Family Night romantic?

Romance is all about communication. Family Night is a chance for the couple to discuss things that might never get discussed. As you each prepare and teach a lesson, you share a part of yourself that often remains hidden. Its great!

What about the kids?

Family Night is all about the whole family. It will help every member of the family feel more a part of the family and more confident in other aspects of life.

To Praise the Parent, Praise the Child

Once after my first child had gone to the doctor for a healthy baby check, my mom asked, "did the doctor tell you how cute your kid is?" She then told me that she would never take her child to a doctor who did not compliment her baby.

Of course, she was just joking with the proud new father. But that little conversation has stuck with me because my mom ended up teaching me an important lesson. As parents, we are highly invested in our kids. Their successes are our success and their failures are our failures. It's natural that parents feel that way because we sacrifice so much for their training and up bringing. When

---

[1] http://lds.org/hf/fhe/welcome/0,16785,4210-1,00.html

123

someone compliments the child, they are also complimenting the parent for doing such a good job in raising the child.

Remember to compliment your children yourself. Compliment them sincerely for things they do well. Also, compliment them in ways that reflect well on your partner. Each of us see certain aspects of ourselves in our kids. Compliment your child on those things.

Romance and Children

Some feel that when the children arrive, the romance of marriage is over. Children take so much time and attention that it is hard to even find a spare moment to be together for anything. Romance seems out of the question. As the kids get older, the demands change and its becomes harder and harder to be romantic. Yet hope is not lost.

Think of the kids as your little romantic army. When you are doing something romantic for your sweetie, plan a way for the kids to participate in at least part of it. An idea of how to do this is mentioned in Family Romance (see page 119). When preparing breakfast in bed for that special someone, let the kids do some of the cooking or write a "We love you" card.

By including the kids you will emphasize the message you are trying to send to your sweetie. When you take all the effort of getting the kids to help it adds to the feeling of love and gratitude. Beside, the kids love it.

Safety First

An article called blackout (see page 121) suggested having a pretend blackout. It can be a lot of fun, especially if you tell family stories or stories of your childhood around a small light. Our children really eat it up.

The tip for today is to go over one of the **safety checklists** from the **Safety Tip** page at the Safe Kids website[1]. Be sure and make it fun. Maybe a practice fire drill with everyone crawling on the ground with blindfolds on to simulate a house full of smoke.

Its not a very romantic topic, I admit. But saving a life or preventing an accident can be very romantic.

---

[1] http://www.safekids.org/

Getting Messy

Ever notice how much fun kids have getting messy? They are attracted to puddles and mud like moths to a flame. For some good dirty fun let out that inner kid out. Go for a walk in the rain, splash and laugh. Maybe have a whipping cream fight or make a cake with plenty of powdered sugar and chocolate.

Be an All-Pro Dad

Romance comes from being attracted to each other. Did you know that one thing women find attractive is confidence? Its true. If you are confident in yourself and your abilities, that confidence will make your sweetie less stressed. Less stress means she is feeling better about herself and your relationship.

One way to build confidence in ones abilities is to improve those abilities. How can you improve in your roles as husband and father? At AllProDad.com[1] they have a mailing list with advice for fathers. The advice runs the whole gambit. Some of it is useful and some less so. On the whole, its great way to add some tools and advice to your fathering toolbox.

Support our Troops

Whether you support the war in Iraq or not, the soldiers serving there deserve our support. Most of us have a neighbor, friend or relative serving overseas. Why not spend some time together doing something for those soldiers.? See Any Soldier[2] for ideas of what to send. They also can help if you want to send a package but don't know any soldiers personally.

Hoopla

We like to play different board and card games. Its a great way to pass some family time or even just the two of you. The downside to most games is that

---

[1] http://www.allprodad.com/
[2] http://www.anysoldier.us/WhatToSend.html

they are competitive. That is, if one of you wins, the other must lose. There is nothing wrong with that really. Life is just like that.

As fun as being competitive is, its often more enjoyable and more rewarding to work together. That is where Hoopla comes in. Rather than competing against each other, all the players make a single team trying to complete a given number of tasks in a certain amount of time. The game consists of a bunch of cards with something on them. There is also a die with colors instead of numbers. Also included is a wind up timer.

On your turn you roll the dice. The task is determined by the color that shows. Each task consists on getting the other members of your team to guess what is on your card. The color determines how you give the clues. One color means to draw it, another means to act it out without talking, another allows you to use any word not included on the card but all the words must begin with the same letter. There are others but I'll save them as a surprise.

This is a great game in a couple of ways. First, it teaches you and your family to work together to solve problems. Second, the timer is set for fifteen minutes meaning it won't take all night to play. Finally, it is just plain fun.

The one drawback I've noticed is that my youngest (eight years old) doesn't know what all the words mean. She likes to play anyway. We just added the rule that if she doesn't know what the word means she can add the card back into the deck and get another card. For the younger crowd, try Cadoo instead.

Anticipating Star Wars

I was reading in the paper about some of the people camped out for a week in line to see the latest Star Wars. Its was wet here so people waiting in line had to camp out in the rain. There were even some families there, with all the kids. When asked why they were doing it, they responded that this is the last time, the end of an era. It was something the family would remember for a long time.

Although Star Wars may not be your thing, do something to make some memories. Family vacations or the romantic getaway are good memory makers. Sitting in line for Star Wars and meeting new people in the process also seems to work.

There are lots of other opportunities to make lasting memories. Most community and charitable organizations need volunteers. Even if you can't sing or act, the local theater could use stage crew help. Maybe take a class together.

The city is registering for their summer program. Maybe a dance class or a dutch-oven cooking class together.

Camping

Before we talked about making S'Mores (see page 73) and how you don't need to be camping to enjoy these tasty treats. Of course, s'mores and camping go hand in hand. Everything seems to taste better cooked in the great outdoors, even marshmallows.

Camping is a great way to bring some fire into a relationship. As much as I love the campfire and smelling like smoke, I'm talking about the other kind of fire, the romantic one. Going camping is a nice trip outside the comfort zone. Everything about life is changed. Even the most common and everyday tasks become an adventure. This includes everything from sleeping, to cooking and even the outhouse. For a short while, nothing is boring because everything is different.

Also, you end up with a lot of free time on your hands. Everything seems to take longer so you have more time to spend together doing tasks like cooking. Besides, there is no TV to interrupt your conversations.

Even if you can't go camping, try sleeping outside a night or two, maybe even under the stars. Or just pull out the sleeping bags and camp out in the living room.

Holding the Door Open

I must admit it. The truth is I rarely hold the car door open for my wife anymore. When we were dating and first married, she would even wait for me to come around and open it for her. It was all so very romantic. Then kids came. With car seats, diaper bags and everything else, running around and opening the door when she would just have to get out and wrangle a kid or two seemed pointless.

The final end came with our latest vehicle. The lock on the passenger side door doesn't work from the outside. I have to open the driver side door and unlock the other doors. By the time I get back around, she's already inside, belt buckled and wondering what the hold up is.

Only for special date nights do we allow the extra time for me to open the door for her. How much time is it? Oh, about five seconds. Yet we are always in a hurry to get somewhere and those few moments seem like an eternity.

More's the pity because my children have not seen me make the effort to show my wife that extra little bit of courtesy. Its very important for them to see a good example of love, respect and courtesy from their parents so they know how to treat their future spouses, and how they should expect to be treated.

Guys: Make the effort to do the traditional courtesies like holding doors, carrying things and so forth.

Gals: Give your sweetie the opportunity to show a good example to your kids. Graciously accept the courtesies with a sincere thanks you.

Keys to a Successful Marriage

From the Declaration on the Family: "Successful marriages and families are established and maintained on principles of faith, prayer, repentance, forgiveness, respect, love, compassion, work, and wholesome recreational activities."

Incorpoate each of these attributes in your life together. One way to get started is to pick one and work on it for a week. Hopefully by the end of a week it will have become a habit, then pick the next one and start working on it. Make a point of working on your marriage a little bit everyday.

Coaching

Once upon a time, my daughter's soccer coach was out of town, so he asked me to fill in for him. I was happy to do so having coached her team for a couple of years previously. Being coach for a day reminded me of what a great opportunity coaching my daughter's team is to build a relationship with her. On top of that, its a great tool for keeping the fire going between me and my sweetie.

When you coach a team, you get more involved in your child's life in a positive way. You don't even need to be a great coach, just put your heart into it and do your best. You get to spend time with your child and their friends. During the course of the season, you will meet many of the parents of your child's friends. Of course, your will develop an extra bond of love and shared experiences with your child. Besides, its great fun.

Its not just the guys who can coach. There are a lot of gals who coach as well.

Where does your spouse fit in? Its impossible to coach a team alone. Its a lot like herding cats some days. Your sweetie can also be involved with the peripheral activities that go on like leading the cheering section, rounding up the stragglers, and showing support. I've found it a wonderful way to break out of the comfort zone and have some positive shared experiences as a couple. Thanks for your help, sweetie!

Of course, coaching youth sports is not the only way to have these sorts of experiences. Most youth organizations need adult volunteers. These organizations include:

- youth sports
- scouting (cub, boy or girl scouts)
- school clubs
- PTA

Spend some time not just being a parent, but being a coach as well.

Teaching Gratitude

Romance and Children (see page 124) talks about involving your children with the romantic gestures you show your sweetie. By involving your little helpers, they get to enjoy the experience, but they are also learning from your example and your wisdom. Today, let's take that a step further and teach the children to be more grateful.

My wife does a lot and sacrifices a lot for me and the kids. Being a stay at home mom, she ends up doing a lot of thankless jobs. Why are they thankless? Because nobody bothers to thank her, of course. Its not that the tasks are not important, because they are. It is just that she does them and so nobody else notices. What's worse, the kids are often grumpy and disrespectful to my wife.

How can you teach the kids to be grateful and respectful? Make a game of it like is mentioned in the Twenty-five Days of Thanksgiving (see page 103).

Another game would be to have the kids write down every nice thing that mom does for them and collect them in a jar for a week or two. At the end of the time, have a small celebration in your sweetheart's honor. Give her the jar along with a gift certificate for something she really enjoys but isn't normally able to take the time to enjoy. For my wife, that might be a massage. Also arrange the time for her to do it.

Hidden Messages

We have been remodeling the basement. The previous owners had had a flood in the basement, but had not taken care of it. Turns out there was a bunch of mold starting at the floor and going up to the about three feet on all the drywall. I am having to tear out drywall and redo some framing. Fortunately the mold is all taken care of now and the rebuilding has commenced.

As I was admiring our handy work, it occurred to me that we are going to be enjoying and using these wall for many years to come. Its not like the walls are going anywhere and we have no plans to move. In the future we can share and remember this time. The memories made all the more precious by the hard work it took to make it all happen.

We are going to make it a bit more romantic by adding a time capsule somewhere in one of the walls. Included will be a love note from each of us. That way when we see that section of the wall, we will be reminded of our love for each other. Nobody will every see or read them once the wall is sealed, but we will know they are there.

Eating Together Regularly

Our lives are busy. Work, chores, homework and errands all work to minimize the amount of time we have to ourselves. Sometimes it is just a chore to find time to eat, let alone do it together on regular schedule.

Now think back to the time you spent courting your sweetheart. How many of your dates revolved around food and eating? Dinner and a movie, picnic in the park, or a shared ice cream sundae? One of the turning points in our courtship is when I cooked for my girlfriend and future wife for the first time. I worked hard to set an elegant mood and prepared the best meal I could. My swegirlfriend etheart really appreciated it and we spent a wonderful meal together.

Eating together seems to be an important aspect of human relationships. Even at work we "do lunch" when we want to spend time together. How much more important should it be with the love your life?

Work hard to schedule evening meals together as a couple. Might be a good idea to turn off the TV so you can talk as a couple or as a family. Then, for a special treat, take time to have lunch together. Its one of the most romantic things you can do.

Money Can Be Romantic

We all have heard the statistics concerning divorce and finances. Talking about money can be tricky. For some reason, people are easily offended when money is the topic.

Some ideas to make talking about money easier:

- Do not talk about money when tired
- Write down the decisions so you don't have to remake them
- Don't wait until there is a problem.

Most important is to talk about money regularly so it does not become a big problem.

Living Under the Time Pressure

At work I have a calendar on the computer that keeps my schedule and lets everyone else know if I am in meetings or otherwise not available. This allows me to plan my time and also manage the expectations of others. People know I won't be at my desk if my calendar says I'm in a meeting. It also keeps people from double booking meetings. My time at work is very precious and needs to be managed accordingly.

One thing I do is schedule an hour a day for excersise. This simple act ensures that no meeting is schedule at that time. The computer even reminds me when its time to go workout.

Isn't your time with your family no less important than your time at work? Find ways to schedule your personal life the same way you schedule your work life. When all is said and done, your relationship with your spouse is far more important than your work or career. If need be, I will put an "appointment" with my sweetheart into my calendar at work, just to make sure that nothing conflicts with that important appointment.

Homework Assignment

My daughter had a home work assignment. I don't recall if it was for health or English class, but that doesn't really matter. The assignment was to interview a parent (or guardian) about dating. Come to think of it, it was health.

Anyway, there were several question she was to ask and we, as parents, had to answer. Reading the questions brought back some fun memories for me, so I decided to share the questions so you can share them with your sweetie.

1. Where did you go on your very first date? What did you do?

2. Where did you go on your first date with your sweetie?

3. What did you do?

4. At what age did you start dating?

5. How long did you and your sweetheart date before getting married?

6. When did you know you were going to get married?

7. What was the best date you ever went on?

8. What was the worst date ever?

9. What would you like to do on a date that you have never done before?

New Mailing List: ferociousflirting

As much fun creating the *Romantic Tips for Married Couples* website has been, its time to take it to the next step. I have spent years studying good relationships and practicing in my own marriage. This has given me a lot of good ideas and good experiences that I can share.

But I do not have the corner on the market on positive experiences and good ideas. That is where you come in. Subscribe to the ferociousflirting mailing list[1] and share your experiences and ideas with other like-minded couples.

The mailing list has these features:

- The discussion on the list is in the G or PG range (it is meant for adults to share ideas in a family-friendly way)
- The list is moderated to ensure that the discussion remains relevant, positive and friendly—no foul language or obscene posts
- Spam will not be tolerated
- Only people who join the list will be allowed to post (this helps keep the noise to a minimum)

If you have a great marriage already, please come and share your successes and ideas. If you want to put the fire back into your relationship then join in, ask questions and take advantage of the experiences of others.

The final word

I love you, sweetheart!

---

[1] http://groups.yahoo.com/subscribe/ferociousflirting